FEARLESS

Pray More

Janet Ramsdell Rockey

FEARLESS
Pray More

A Woman's
Devotional Guide to
Courageous Living

BARBOUR BOOKS
An Imprint of Barbour Publishing, Inc.

Published by Barbour Books, an imprint of Publishing, Inc., P.O. Box 719, Uhrichsville,
Ohio 44683, www.barbourbooks.com

*Our mission is to publish and distribute inspirational products offering exceptional value and
biblical encouragement to the masses.*

Member of the
Evangelical Christian
Publishers Association

Printed in the United States of America.

Introduction

Let those who fear the Lord now say,
"His mercy endures forever."
PSALM 118:4 NKJV

Fear is an alarming emotion caused by a belief that someone or something is likely to cause harm, pain, or present a threat to us or our loved ones.

The Bible uses two connotations of the same word, which overlap in definition. We who fear the Lord have a humbling respect for His magnificence. We are also afraid of what He could do to us, if not for His immeasurable grace.

A live wire hopping on the ground, shooting sparks in all directions, causes us take a few steps back. We remain safe when we acknowledge its deadly power. Electricity has no mercy.

By the same token, if we fear the Lord in reverence, then we have no reason to cower in fear of His wrath. We believe He sent His Son, Jesus, to take the death sentence meant for us.

Heavenly Father, how liberating to know that we can
dwell in Your loving presence where fear has no power
over us because Your mercy endures forever!

5

Courage in Devilish Ant Bites

*"Do not fear them, for the Lord
your God is the one fighting for you."*
Deuteronomy 3:22 nasb

Traffic delays, misplaced items, command of the remote control
. . .are only a few of my everyday devil's ant bites.

These minor irritations, piled upon one another, produce
mountains of frustration. My husband's rare victory for the
remote control provides a great analogy: football.

In American football, the object of the game is to move the
ball downfield to the goalpost. Your offensive line gains eight
yards. Their defensive line pushes you back ten. You throw
the ball to a teammate. They intercept it and advance toward
their goalpost.

Such is our daily scrimmage with the devil's ant bites. Each
incident of advance and retreat can leave us exasperated, unless
we give it to the Lord. When we realize He is willing to fight
for us before we engage in the skirmish, the enemy is defeated.

*Dear Lord, You have provided broadcasts of biblical
teaching during traffic delays, answered my prayer for
misplaced items, and offered a life lesson in my husband's
choice of programming. Thank You for fighting for me.*

Courage in His Shadow

*Now you don't need to be afraid of the
dark anymore, nor fear the dangers of the day.*

PSALM 91:5 TLB

During a trip to visit my sister, my husband and I took a tour of
a cavern park nearby. We sat on a bench inside the cave, waiting
for the scheduled lightshow to begin. The pointed stalactites
hanging from the ceiling resembled giant teeth, ready to devour
us. Then all the lights went out. Pitch darkness pressed around
me. I gripped my husband's hand. The show had begun.

In total darkness, we can't perceive direction. Our sense of
balance—as well as security—is lost. Danger might be lurking
right next to us.

The biblical theme of that lightshow reminded me that I
have no need to fear the dark. Since the day I believed in Jesus
Christ as my Savior, the only darkness in my life is the shadow
of the Most High.

*O Holy God, Your faithfulness is a
permanent shield and fortress. Thank You
for Your promise to be a light in our dark days.*

Whom Shall I Fear

Fear lives next door to faith.

David's personal testimony proves he was serious about praising the Lord, yet he still pleaded with God not to hide His face from him. David's enemies stumbled and fell when they came against him, yet he asked the Lord to not deliver him into their hands. He knew God wouldn't abandon him in the days of trouble, yet his one desire was to dwell in God's presence every moment.

Like David, our one desire in life should be to dwell in God's three-fold presence all the days of our lives. In God's omnipresence, we see Him everywhere we look. He dwells in us as the Holy Spirit the moment we believe in Christ, and He will never leave us. In His manifest presence, His embracing calmness soothes our souls in our darkest moments.

*Teach us, O Lord, to focus on our faith in You
and see Your goodness in the land of the living.*

Victim or Victor—the Courage to Choose

The horse is prepared for the day of battle,
but victory belongs to the Lord.
Proverbs 21:31 NASB

The first therapeutic step after encountering a crime is to make an important decision. Do we want to cower and remain the victim, or take action and be the victor? Whether we've suffered at the hands of a bully, a scammer, or a violent criminal, facing the offender takes great courage.

As the Philistines victimized the Israelites, David's faith in the Lord gave him courage to confront Goliath. "'The Lord zzzwho delivered me from the paw of the lion and from the paw of the bear, He will deliver me from the hand of this Philistine'" (1 Samuel 17:37 NASB).

We all have a Goliath to face. Confronting a bully, apprehending a con artist, or testifying against an assailant. God provided the right stone to make David the victor instead of the victim. Our stone is the Rock, which is Christ the Lord.

Father, as we prepare to fight our Goliaths,
help us choose to be the victor. For we know if
we want victory, we can't fight without You.

Fear of Unanswered Prayer

Wait for the LORD; be strong and let your
heart take courage; yes, wait for the LORD.
PSALM 27:14 NASB

In the middle of my workday several years ago, I realized I hadn't yet said my good morning to the Lord. My C.A.T.S. prayer (Confession, Adoration, Thanksgiving, and Supplication) had slipped into a "sometimes" rather than daily prayer. I asked God to remind me to greet Him every morning.

The next morning, I awoke with a hymn going through my mind. More than ten years later, I still wake up to the song of His choice. I hum a few bars and say, "Good morning, Lord. How can I serve You today?"

During a recent medical crisis, I expected an immediate answer to my prayers. But nothing changed. In my distress, I wondered if my prayers bounced back from the ceiling. Then the soft melody of the hymn, "Under His Wings," floated through my mind, giving me strength and encouragement.

God reminded me He answers all our prayers—in His own time.

O Lord, how I rejoice as I pray and wait for You to act!

Fear of Running Out of Gas

*For consider Him who endured such hostility
from sinners against Himself, lest you become
weary and discouraged in your souls.*

HEBREWS 12:3 NKJV

When the tiny gas tank on my dashboard lights up, I immediately look for a service station. A previously broken fuel gauge made me aware that cars don't run on empty.

Neither do we.

Christ's disciples must've experienced "low fuel" moments. Peter's spiritual gauge probably dropped below empty when Jesus looked at him after the rooster crowed. Peter bitterly wept.

God has provided gauges within our souls to warn us that we're nearly empty. They're as obvious as a dashboard light, if we remain alert. We neglect fellowship with believers and spend less time reading the Bible. Soured attitudes and lame excuses follow.

When discouragement sneaks in, it's possibly a warning light on our spiritual dashboard. We can call a friend from church, open the Bible, and pray for the Lord to refuel our tanks. He won't leave us stranded without hope.

*Father God, thank You for not leaving us on empty.
We have an everlasting fuel supply through Your love.*

Fear of the Should-Haves

*Therefore, keep up your courage, men, for I believe
God that it will turn out exactly as I have been told.*
ACTS 27:25 NASB

The words, "You should have. . ." are not easy to hear. They usually invoke a humble response of, "I was wrong." Those words are not always easy to say. We are blind to the future, but hindsight has 20/20 vision.

Paul warned the centurion who was in charge of him that impending danger lay ahead of the voyage. But the centurion listened to the captain and the pilot instead. They made their decision to sail based on the condition of the harbor, instead of listening to Paul, who had God's ear.

Although Paul said, "You should have listened to me," he encouraged the men because God sent an angel to disclose that all lives on board would be spared. God's plan included Paul being shipwrecked before going to Rome.

*Almighty God, when we face a dreaded "should have,"
let us remember that You are still in control. As with Paul, You
will use every situation to bring about Your plan for us.*

Courage in the Light

*"The people who sat in darkness have seen a
great light, and upon those who sat in the region
and shadow of death Light has dawned."*
MATTHEW 4:16 NKJV

Two weeks without sunshine during a Texas Panhandle winter put me in a dreadful mood. Constant cloud coverage, heavy with snow, made the drab winter days neither light nor dark, but a dreary shade of gray.

As much as we need sunlight to maintain our physical and mental health, we need "Son light" more to care for our spiritual well-being.

Jesus said, "'I am the Light of the world; he who follows Me will not walk in the darkness, but will have the Light of life'" (John 8:12 NASB). With Him as our light, nothing is hidden; everything is in view. We can find joy in the drab and gray moments because He is always with us.

In sunshine or clouds, in night or day, let us praise the Lord, for our Light has dawned.

*Gracious God, the light and presence of our Savior give us the
courage to face life's dreary days. Whom shall we fear?*

Courage to Accept Criticism

Don't refuse to accept criticism; get all the help you can.
PROVERBS 23:12 TLB

Arriving at my first writers' conference, I learned the only thing I had correct was the font. I gasped at the words, *Come see me*, a faculty member had written on my manuscript. A professional writer wanted to discuss my work! I felt like a schoolgirl getting called to the principal's office.

When I met with her, she told me why she hated the love interest character in my romance novel. Her opinion made sense. Her carefully asked questions helped me create a more believable storyline.

I admit I'm not that eager to accept suggestions from my husband while I'm driving. He likewise rejects my advice when he's behind the wheel. Criticism is like a large pill, but offering it in kindness and love makes it easier to swallow.

We won't learn and grow if we aren't aware of our mistakes.

Precious Lord, thank You for the critiques and assessments that teach us to improve ourselves in every task we do. For we do them all for You.

Courage to Write

"Oh that my words were written! Oh that they were inscribed in a book! That with an iron stylus and lead they were engraved in the rock forever!"
JOB 19:23–24 NASB

One Saturday every month, I meet with a group of Christian writers to critique and encourage each other in our quests to write for the Lord. We see an assortment of genres, from fiction novels to devotionals to memoirs.

During my first meeting, I sat in awe of the successful, published authors in my small group. They offered their expertise to bolster us "newbies" on our journeys. As we studied the craft, our confidence and courage to write grew.

Job wished to write about the glory of the Lord, even in his agony. While it is unknown who actually authored this book of the Bible, we know the Lord guided the stylus to tell Job's story of loss, suffering, and restoration. We can trust His guidance in our work, too.

Lord God, the tapestry of our words is carefully stitched to tell of Your glories. Your will is handwoven through the stories of our lives.

Fear of Deadlines

*Remembering that it is the Lord Christ who is going
to pay you, giving you your full portion of all he owns.
He is the one you are really working for.*

<small>Colossians 3:24 tlb</small>

Nothing gives me sweaty palms like an approaching deadline—especially from an outside source. I've set a deadline for myself, but a friend always has a party, out-of-town family members drop in, or my husband invites the neighbors to supper. My personal deadline becomes more and more flexible as I move it farther and farther down the calendar. Flexibility isn't an option when a boss or publisher sets the cut-off date, but distractions still prevail.

Interruptions are a deadline's worst enemy, so I created a self-motivating motto:

> *If you shirk God's work for a day of play,
> There is twice the price you'll have to pay.*

Christ has called us to do the chore. Let us not shirk His work, but take courage to face our deadline—and finish the job.

*Regardless of the task You've given us, Lord God, we trust You
will help us stay focused as we prayerfully rely on You.*

Fear of the Empty Nest

"Do not fear, for I am with you; I will bring your offspring from the east, and gather you from the west."

ISAIAH 43:5 NASB

Eager to spread my wings and explore the world, I left the nest as a fledgling at the age of seventeen. Being underage, the law forced me to move back home. By the time I reached my twenties, my dad considered installing a revolving door to our home. I had become a seasoned flyer while still trying to establish my independence.

Whether sending off fledglings or seasoned flyers, parents' hearts fear, yet swell with pride, when their children grow up and leave the nest. Like teaching a child to ride a bike, we won't let go of the handlebar until we're sure they've got their balance. What better balance can we give them but the Word of God? Like John, we have no greater joy than to hear of our children walking in the truth.

Heavenly Father, as You bring our offspring back to the nest from time to time, let our joy be complete when they return with hearts full of Your love.

Silence—Dread or Delight

A time to keep silence, and a time to speak. . .
ECCLESIASTES 3:7 NKJV

What does it mean when all the crickets in the night become silent? Danger.

All creatures hush their activities when evil lurks, or so it seems in movies. It could mean we should prepare for the dispensing of judgment, as in the thirty minutes of silence when the Lamb breaks the seventh seal.

Let us instead find delight in silence, a welcome relief after a busy day filled with beeping machines and talkative people, followed by honking traffic.

The first thing I do when I get home from work is turn off the radio my husband listens to while he's cooking dinner. He likes the chatter of talk radio. I want peace and quiet. Silence is golden.

God has assigned the moments of silence and sounds. We can overcome our dread of silence in His Word. As His children, we have no fear of the judgment to come. We can delight in the quiet assurance of His forgiveness.

Dear God, our souls wait in silence for
from You only comes our salvation.

Fear of Having Authority over Others

And Jesus came and spoke to them, saying, "All authority has been given to Me in heaven and on earth."
MATTHEW 28:18 NKJV

I was only thirty-five when my new boss pointed at me and said, "You're now the supervisor." As a secretary with the company only a few weeks, I wondered, *Why me?* What made him think I could take charge of the other secretaries? The thought of being a boss petrified me. What if I had to fire someone? After praying about it, I felt comfortable accepting my new responsibilities and title. It was an opportunity for the Lord to work through me—my mission field!

When Jesus presented the Great Commission to the eleven disciples, He passed the baton of authority to them. They were the new bosses, yet were still under Christ's power. They could heal the sick, make the lame walk and the deaf hear, but only in His name.

*Almighty God, as we govern or manage others,
let us remember that You are the true source of our
authority and to show mercy where mercy is due.*

Fear of Retirement

"After retirement they can assist with various light duties in the
Tabernacle, but will have no regular responsibilities."
NUMBERS 8:26 TLB

After thirty years of work, my friend decided to retire. But every month she found another reason to stay a little longer. She dreaded the day when she would no longer awake at the crack of dawn to go to work.

Most of us look forward to a time of unlimited leisure, until retirement stares us in the face. The emptiness of a blank day yawns at us as we imagine sitting in a rocker with nothing to do. Yet those empty moments immediately fill up with to-do lists, hobbies, and friends in need.

Like the Levite priests, we can still perform light duties for the church when age slows us down. We can find many small jobs in the Lord's service, like offering someone unable to drive a ride to church. A shut-in might enjoy a home-cooked meal . . .or a dessert.

God our Father, as we fear the final closing of
the door to our workplaces, remind us that there
is no full retirement from Your service.

Fear of Limitations

The LORD said to Moses, "Is the LORD's power limited? Now you shall see whether My word will come true for you or not."
NUMBERS 11:23 NASB

Is the sky the limit? I've heard that promise all my life. Yet, life's limitations have grounded me many times. Limited funds prevented large-priced purchases. My career advancement was stalled by my limited education. My age puts limits on some of the activities I could do when I was a younger woman. Either the sky really isn't the limit, as the adage claims, or my sky fell years ago.

The Israelites thought they had their share of limits. They complained to Moses, saying God's manna wasn't enough to satisfy their hunger. Moses complained to the Lord, saying he wasn't strong enough to cope with the belligerent people. Both doubted God's limitless power.

We have physical limitations in this mortal life. But there is no limit to the expanse of God's love for us. He gave His only begotten Son that we should not perish, but have eternal life.

*Almighty God, nothing we can do will
match Your unlimited love for us.*

Courage to Answer God's Calling

The angel said to her, "Do not be afraid, Mary;
for you have found favor with God."
LUKE 1:30 NASB

My Great Aunt Emily accepted the call from God to minister to the people in China in the 1930s. I inherited the poem her mother wrote, offering her child to God.

God's calling could be as simple as speaking to someone on an airplane. One of our pastors had called his wife from the jetliner to let her know his flight was delayed. Her reply was, "Who is sitting next to you?" He accepted the opportunity to chat with the person next to him about the Lord.

God's calling could be as big as a request from a publisher to write a devotional, or as small as a lunch date with a family member. We do know it won't be to birth the Son of God, Mary already accepted that calling. We can learn from her obedient faith. When the angel explained how it would happen, Mary replied, "'May it be done to me according to your word'" (Luke 1:38 NASB).

Heavenly Father, when You call, may we
do Your will according to Your Word.

Courage in Teaching

Come, you children, listen to me;
I will teach you the fear of the LORD.
PSALM 34:11 NASB

A teacher once told me she was on the front lines. How sad that she views her students as the enemy. The classroom should never resemble a battleground, although it often does.

A principal put all his most difficult students in one classroom. It reminded me of the film, *The Great Escape*. The Nazis housed all their notorious escapists in the same camp. Their plan backfired. Nearly eighty prisoners escaped. Would the principal's plan also go awry?

The petite young woman whom he transferred in to teach the filthy-mouthed, angry preteens viewed her assignment as a divine appointment. Along with the required coursework, she would show them Jesus.

"They won't fire me," she said, "because no other teacher will take these children."

She showed no fear—only Christ's love. By the third week of school, the profanity had nearly stopped. She'd earned their respect.

Precious Lord, Jesus admonishes us not to
hinder the children from coming to Him. Give our
teachers the courage to teach about Your love.

Courage to Seek Wisdom

"For wisdom is better than jewels; and all
desirable things cannot compare with her."
PROVERBS 8:11 NASB

What is the difference between knowledge and wisdom? We find knowledge in textbooks, but wisdom only comes from the word of the Lord.

When God offered Solomon anything he wanted, the new king asked only for an understanding heart to discern between good and evil. Because Solomon asked in humility, God blessed him with wisdom as plentiful as sand on the seashore. He also rewarded him with great wealth, honor, and a long life.

We need knowledge to get through life. Reading, writing, and arithmetic provide the milk of our learning. But the meat of wisdom brings honor. If we remain content with mere book knowledge, we lose the joy of serving Him. But when we seek wisdom as though seeking silver, searching for it as for hidden treasure, then He will reward us with unexpected, incomparable blessings—better than jewels.

O Lord our God, let wisdom enter our hearts
and bring pleasure to our souls that we may use these
divine gifts to serve You with glory and honor.

Fear of Ignorance

*For they being ignorant of God's righteousness,
and seeking to establish their own righteousness,
have not submitted to the righteousness of God.*

ROMANS 10:3 NKJV

Those who worship the false gods of this world claim to be wise. But they show their ignorance when they call Christians "knuckle-draggers" or "flat-earthers." How can they say we are descended from the knuckle-dragging ape when we believe mankind was created in the image of God? The Bible describes the earth as a circle in Isaiah 40:22. How then can they accuse Christians of once believing the earth was flat?

They say we are anti-science, yet archeologists find proof of biblical accounts in the ancient tells of Israel and other parts of the Middle East region.

In their fear of ignorance, they point accusing fingers at us, not realizing they're actually pointing to themselves. Sadly, they will remain in their fear of ignorance until they submit to the righteousness of God through the Lord Jesus Christ.

*Father God, please open the eyes of nonbelievers to
Your righteousness. Give us the courage to teach
them that wisdom comes from knowing You.*

Courage to Contend with Bullies

"But I tell you not to resist an evil person. But whoever slaps you on your right cheek, turn the other to him also."
MATTHEW 5:39 NKJV

The scene in a Christmas film with a bully terrorizing his classmates made an interesting point. The boy's favorite victim, Ralphie, became a bully himself when he used his fists to quash his enemy. But is that the way the Lord would have us contend with our oppressors?

A bully isn't always the tough kid who beats up other children. For adults, it could be a tyrannical boss, a domineering spouse, or even a pushy, well-meaning friend.

Jesus' example of responding with an attitude of kindness or a gentle answer would unsettle them more than if we'd shouted or raised a hand at them. If we love our enemies and pray for those who persecute us, then we have contended with our bullies in a way that pleases the Lord.

*Gracious God, give us courage when bullies
come against us to show Your love in such a way
that they will open their hearts to You.*

Courage to Submit to Authority

For rulers are not a cause of fear for good behavior,
but for evil. Do you want to have no fear of authority?
Do what is good and you will have praise from the same.
ROMANS 13:3 NASB

Protestors refuse to accept a newly elected president. Rioters throw rocks and bottles at police. Students disregard their teachers' directives. These are only a few examples of our failure to respect authority of any kind.

God established the principle of government to maintain order. In resisting those in authority over us, we oppose the ordinance of God and will be accorded the consequences.

Protocols are in place to handle those who abuse their authority. Impeach, file a complaint, or contact superiors. Riots accomplish nothing but destruction.

Although David had been anointed king, he submitted to Saul's reign, waiting for the Lord's timing. His respect for Saul, a man who attempted to kill David several times, came from his love for God.

Lord, by submitting to the authority You have
set in place, we recognize and revere Your sovereignty.
Let those in power look to You for guidance.

Fear of Confrontation

*"Do not fear or be dismayed; tomorrow go out
to face them, for the Lord is with you."*
2 Chronicles 20:17 NASB

Intimidation has worked in the past. As a youngster, I cowered in fear when a raised voice was aimed at me. An angry stare would tongue-twist any clever comeback I might conjure up. My fear of confrontation followed me into adulthood until God reminded me that I'm not a doormat. I am His child.

In fear, Jehoshaphat sought the Lord's guidance and protection in the expected attack from his enemies. He proclaimed a nationwide fast, then glorified God before requesting His help.

Chapter 20 in 2 Chronicles gave me new confidence when faced with a dreaded confrontation. I give God the glory, then ask Him to strengthen, guide, and protect me.

Whether confronting a well-meaning friend, a bully, or a fierce enemy, let us turn to the Lord in prayer—first in praise, then in supplication.

*Lord God, we turn to You before facing our enemies
and pray for the right attitude and words, as well as courage
to confront them with Christlike graciousness.*

Fear of Being Vulnerable

*So he said, "I heard Your voice in the garden,
and I was afraid because I was naked; and I hid myself."*
GENESIS 3:10 NKJV

Adam and Eve lost their innocence when they disobeyed God's only commandment to them. This left them vulnerable to new dangers in their environment, dangers that didn't exist before their sin transformed the world.

God used animal skins to protect them from exposure. A sacrificial lamb was the only way out of their predicament. This pointed toward our Father's ultimate solution of covering our sin with the blood of the Lamb, Jesus Christ.

Worldly circumstances thrust us into uncertainty. Alone in a stalled vehicle on a deserted road, a loved one in crisis, even various news reports make us feel weak and helpless. Unlike Adam and Eve, we are not naked. We are covered by His blood. Christ Jesus, who died for our sins, will always be with us. Let us call upon Him to come to our aid.

*Gracious Lord, thank You for Your constant
presence in our lives. Even when we feel alone,
help us to remember You are here.*

Courage to Live in Harmony

*Now may the God of patience and comfort grant you to be
like-minded toward one another, according to Christ Jesus,
that you may with one mind and one mouth glorify the
God and Father of our Lord Jesus Christ.*
ROMANS 15:5–6 NKJV

An orchestra begins with a cacophony of instruments playing
different tunes. To open their performance, the first chair violinist
plays the *A* note. The other musicians then tune their instruments
to that one note to reach the perfect blend of harmony.

God orchestrated His harmony in the Garden of Eden.
Man brought dissonance when he rebelled against his Creator.
Our heavenly Father played the perfect note in His Son, Jesus
Christ. The best way to reach the precise balance of harmony
with Him is by tuning our hearts to His Word.

We can find true harmony when we imitate Christ by putting
others first. Accepting one another as Christ accepts us creates
a soothing melody for life.

*Father God, please grant us the courage to
accept one another, to respond in one accord to
Your perfect note, and to seek to live in harmony.*

Fear of Praise

And each is tested by the praise accorded him.
PROVERBS 27:21 NASB

I met a man who was careful not to praise himself, lest he appear boastful. Instead, he told me about other people's praises of him.

How we respond to accolades is a good assessment of our moral fiber. A fear of praise might bring about a self-deprecating reply, which hints at false pride. Yet we can dislocate a shoulder patting ourselves on the back in agreement.

People applaud our deeds, while God looks at our hearts.

Jesus praised the poor widow, who put all she had into the temple treasury. He also commended Peter for giving the correct answer to the question, "'Who do you say that I am?'" (Mark 8:29 NASB). The eleventh chapter of Hebrews pays tribute to godly men and women all the way back to Abel.

We may accept praise for our good works by humbly giving glory to the Lord. For our abilities to complete the tasks He assigns to us come from Him.

Heavenly Father, let us overcome this fear by
looking to You, and not people, for praise.

Courage in Anonymity

And I was unknown by face to the
churches of Judea which were in Christ.
GALATIANS 1:22 NKJV

We find safety in anonymity. When our sins aren't displayed in public, no one is the wiser to our humanity. That's why it's easier to tell strangers about Christ's love than our own family members. Those who knew us before we put our trust in Jesus would probably view us as hypocrites. They don't trust the change in our lives.

Paul must've been relieved that the churches of Judea didn't know him by sight. His earlier persecution of the Christians would have tainted his message. He could reach more people with the Gospel if they didn't know about his life before Christ blinded him on the road to Damascus. They might not have believed a radical transformation could've been possible for such a sinner saved by grace. Paul used his anonymity well.

Dear God, give us courage to offer the "unseen hand of
kindness" and bless others anonymously. May our love
for You be so evident that at least one stubborn family
member will follow in our footsteps.

Fear of Fame

And the fame of David went out into all lands;
and the LORD brought the fear of him upon all nations.
1 CHRONICLES 14:17 KJV

Broadway and Hollywood are filled with young people seeking fame and fortune in the entertainment world. Athletes strive to be the most famous player on the team. But some of these fame-seekers fear how celebrity will affect their lives.

Public figures are media magnets. They have no privacy and their adoring fans put them on high pedestals and impose unrealistic expectations on them. Fame can bring pride and conceit, causing the fans to lose interest. The celebrity is no longer in demand.

King David's fame might have gone to his head. In his pride, he took many wives. But in humility, he consulted the Lord before every battle.

Although King David's reputation has endured thousands of years, most celebrities' fame today is fleeting. It only lasts one or two generations, and then they're forgotten like yesterday's newspaper.

What a blessing to know our Lord is a famous King forever.

King of kings, Lord of lords, Your fame
will endure to every generation.

Fear of Being Recognized

So Joseph recognized his brothers,
but they did not recognize him.
GENESIS 42:8 NKJV

As a friend pushed her cart through the grocery store, a woman greeted her, saying, "It's so nice to see you again."

My friend responded in kind, but wondered who in the world that woman was. Maybe an old schoolmate who had drastically changed in appearance? Nothing jogged her memory. Being publicly recognized could prove embarrassing.

Although Joseph recognized his brothers, he disguised himself from them. They might not have known him, even without the disguise. He had grown up and prospered, while they had not changed. Before revealing his identity, Joseph heard them express remorse for their earlier cruelty toward him, and he forgave them.

Sometimes we fear being recognized because it might elicit a confession or need of forgiveness. Perhaps my friend's likeness struck a chord in the stranger's heart, a reminder of a past wrong done to or by her.

All-knowing God, as others recognize our flawed
conditions, let us remember Joseph and his brothers,
and the tremendous gift of forgiveness You offer to each of us.

Fear of Insignificance

So do not fear; you are more valuable than many sparrows.
MATTHEW 10:31 NASB

Jesus sent forth His apostles as sheep in the midst of wolves to bear His message. A plentiful harvest of souls must have seemed insurmountable to the twelve men, giving them reason to fear their own irrelevance.

Like the apostles, we might fear our insignificance in the world system. I've suffered a near-anxiety attack while waiting hours in a long line for assistance. I feared no one cared about my needs. Was I a person, or merely a faceless number to a harried clerk? But then I remembered the sparrow.

God loves the little sparrow, a humble sacrifice for the poor who couldn't afford a lamb, and yet He values us more than that tiny bird. None of us are unimportant to our Creator. He knows how many hairs are on our heads and has a purpose for each of us.

*Lord God, remind us of the lowly sparrow when we
fear being insignificant, so we may remember
that You love us with an everlasting love.*

Fear of Being Forgotten

*"If, when reaping your harvest, you forget to bring
in a sheaf from the field, don't go back after it.
Leave it for the migrants, orphans, and widows."*
DEUTERONOMY 24:19 TLB

In my child psychology class in college, I recognized myself in the description of the forgotten child syndrome.

Parents hover over the first-born child, sometimes called the "experimental child." When the second baby arrives, they have more confidence. By the third child, the parents are so busy with the other two children that they forget to teach him or her the basics of life. These "forgotten children" are taught by their older siblings or must learn by their own experiences.

Since I was the third, and last-born, of my family, this class opened my eyes to the difficulties I experienced during my childhood. What a relief to know I wasn't a slow learner, just a forgotten one.

*Merciful Father, You have not forgotten anyone. You created
each of us for a purpose—to bring glory to Your name.
Let us be the forgotten sheaf in the field to fulfill Your purpose.*

Courage to Be Remembered

*And he was saying, "Jesus, remember
me when You come in Your kingdom!"*

LUKE 23:42 NASB

I ducked behind a kiosk when I saw a former acquaintance. She
continued on her way as I pretended to read the mall directory.
We had shared an apartment many years ago, before I chose
to follow Christ. I feared if she saw me, she would recall those
times of ugliness—times I'd prefer remained forgotten.

We don't want to remember our failings and shortcomings,
and we especially don't want anyone from our past to dredge
them up.

The thief on the cross asked Jesus to remember him when
He entered His kingdom. Not to remember the man's checkered
past or crimes he'd committed, but that he feared God and
believed in Christ.

God looks at us through the filter of Jesus' sacrifice, which
washed away our sin. He remembers us only as His children,
cleansed of our unrighteousness. Let that truth give us courage
to be remembered.

*Merciful Father, we don't need to hide in fear lest You
remember our past, but rejoice because Jesus wiped it clean.*

Fear of Rejection

*He is despised and rejected of men; a man
of sorrows, and acquainted with grief.*
ISAIAH 53:3 KJV

Rejection cuts like a knife through the heart.

A prospective employer offers the job to someone else.

Your valuable gift is callously dismissed.

Your spouse turns away from you.

Fear of being rejected prevents us from moving forward to seek a better job, other recipients of our gifts, or a possible reconciliation. For writers, rejection looms with every piece of work we submit. But we keep writing.

As Isaiah prophesied, many people still reject Jesus. Those who scorn Christ offer His work of salvation to their false gods. They callously refuse His precious gift of eternal life. They spurn the love that Jesus offers to His bride—the body of believers.

Jesus prayed, "Let this cup pass from Me," yet He accepted God's will. He didn't permit any fear of rejection to thwart God's plan for salvation.

*O Lord, give us courage in our fear of rejection. Let us
remember the man of sorrows, acquainted with grief—
our Christ, who will never reject us because He first loved us.*

Fear of Acceptance

But in every nation whoever fears Him and
works righteousness is accepted by Him.
ACTS 10:35 NKJV

As we interview for a new position, which do we fear more—that they won't hire us, or that we'll get the job? Their offer means new responsibilities and, often, new coworkers, which might be scarier than being turned down for the job.

Acceptance by this world is three-fold. It's usually based on proper behavior, pleasing appearance, and a positive attitude. One "off day" brings the anxiety that those who witnessed our angry outburst will no longer accept us. Is it any wonder we sometimes fear it?

Paul's persecution of the Christians before heading to Damascus was acceptable by his peers. Then he was beaten, stoned, and imprisoned by some of those same people for preaching the salvation of the Lord through Jesus Christ.

He chose God's acceptance over the world and encourages us to make that same choice. If we turn our fear of acceptance into fear of the Lord, then He will reckon it to us as righteousness.

Loving Father, thank You for accepting us just as we are.

Fear of Abandonment

At my first defense no one supported me, but all
deserted me; may it not be counted against them.
2 TIMOTHY 4:16 NASB

When someone we love abandons us, we might turn so far inward that it's difficult to find the way out. But putting our trust in Christ will give us courage to close that yawning pit of despair before we fall into it. God has given us the choice to either feel abandoned in a crowded room, or cheerful in an empty house.

The world Jesus came to save abandoned Him. Paul's helpers in Asia left him to preach by himself. Jesus asked God to forgive those who crucified Him. Paul prayed that it not be counted against those who deserted him. Can we emulate Jesus and Paul when others forsake us? Healing begins with forgiveness.

People will abandon us, because we are all flawed sinners saved by grace. But the Lord won't desert us. He is only a prayer away.

O Lord our God, we take comfort in Your
promise that You will not abandon Your people,
nor will You forsake Your inheritance.

Courage to End a Relationship

*"Arise! For this matter is your responsibility,
but we will be with you; be courageous and act."*
EZRA 10:4 NASB

The only time in biblical history when God approved of divorce was in the days of Ezra. It must've been heartbreaking for those families, but God had repeatedly admonished the Israelites against marrying foreign wives. The women brought in their false gods, polluting the Israelites' faithfulness to Almighty God.

Shecaniah, the son of Jehiel, confessed to Ezra, "'We have been unfaithful to our God and have married foreign women from the peoples of the land; yet now there is hope for Israel in spite of this'" (Ezra 10:2 NASB).

God is certain that if we take a spouse from a different religion, our faith and worship will weaken. Being unequally yoked, we begin to compromise on the lighter topics, which eat away at the core of our beliefs.

A victim of marital abuse is unequally yoked. A godly man or woman would not harm the spouse the Lord has provided.

God loves us more than He hates divorce.

Lord, grant us courage, strength, and forgiveness in divorce.

Courage to Begin a New Relationship

"I will give you a new heart and put a new spirit
within you; I will take the heart of stone out of
your flesh and give you a heart of flesh."
EZEKIEL 36:26 NKJV

Once burned, twice shy. How can we trust a new relationship when we've suffered a broken heart? A friend wrestled with that self-doubt when he met a lady a year after his divorce. He feared investing his heart in the new relationship. Another betrayal would shatter it to pieces.

His new lady friend was charming, sensitive, and faithful to the Lord. But that also described how his first wife had been when they'd gotten married. How could he be certain the new relationship wouldn't suffer the same fate?

God heals our broken hearts and binds up our wounded spirits. We can trust Him, and not ourselves, to guide us through a new relationship. Putting our hearts in the Lord's care is a good beginning.

Loving Father, as You remove the stones of fear from our
broken hearts, let us continue to trust in You for guidance.

Fear of Being Outnumbered

But the LORD said to him, "Surely I will be with you,
and you shall defeat Midian as one man."
JUDGES 6:16 NASB

God promoted Gideon from farm boy to general of the Israelite army. When he enlisted thirty-two thousand soldiers, the Midianites outnumbered them four to one.

The Lord scaled back the unit letting twenty-two thousand men depart. Ten thousand were still too many, so He downsized again by testing their vigilance. With three hundred men remaining, they were outnumbered four hundred and fifty to one.

They went up on the mountain, each armed only with a trumpet and a clay jar holding a torch inside. Gideon signaled them to blow the trumpets, break the jars, and raise the torches. The Midianites fled.

Our concern isn't how powerful we are, but how powerful God is. When tears come, when disappointment is our friend, when our future looks bleak, when crushing circumstances paralyze us, fear not, for Jesus is with us. Holding tight to that promise, we can face any foe.

Omnipotent Father, we glorify You.
We are never outnumbered when You are with us.

Fear of Being Lost

*"I will seek my lost ones, those who strayed away,
and bring them safely home again."*
EZEKIEL 34:16 TLB

My friend and I feared for our safety when we lost our way driving home from a writers' conference. We reversed our directions on our return trip, but one-way roads detoured us through undiscovered territory. The overcast sky prevented the sun from guiding us in the right direction. We asked a police officer for help. His advice sent us through a harsh-looking neighborhood. Then the gas gauge dipped into the empty zone. The station attendant offered clearer instructions, adding his warning, "Don't stop until you see the interstate."

We can get lost in worldliness when our thoughts or attitudes cloud our judgment. We take a one-way path away from God and fear we can't find our way back. Detours lead us into dangerous areas where we seek advice from strangers. But God is still with us. He alone can disperse the clouds and let the Son shine in to direct our path back to Him.

*We praise You, Lord, for bringing us safely
back home when we stray from You.*

Fear of Being Found

My flesh trembles for fear of You,
and I am afraid of Your judgments.
PSALM 119:120 NKJV

In youthful pride and anger I strayed from the Lord many years ago. The ways of the world had soured my home, breaking up my family. Rather than humble myself and pray and ask God for help, I turned my back to Him.

My conscience continued to nudge me, reminding me how I grieved the Holy Spirit. I continued to lurk in the shadows of my eclipse of faith even with the Spirit's persistent promptings.

I tried to hide from God for fear He would find me and put me to shame. Pride and fear created an encompassing wall of darkness, but God's love shone right through it. His irresistible light gave me courage to come back to Him.

We can't hide from our heavenly Father. He knows our location every minute of every day, patiently awaiting our return to His fellowship.

Heavenly Father, You are long-suffering and merciful.
Remind me to pray for others who have wandered
away to find their way back to Your loving arms.

Fear of Good News

And the angel said unto them, fear not: for, behold, I bring
you good tidings of great joy, which shall be to all people.
LUKE 2:10 KJV

The shepherds watching their flock that night thought their
evening would be like any other. Lying in the grass, gazing up
at the sky. The stars must've been bright in the darkness. Only
the occasional bleating of sheep disturbed the quiet in the field.

Then the angel appeared, and the glory of the Lord lit up
the pasture.

Good news means change. Jesus' birth radically transformed
how people would relate to God. The religious leaders of that
day were comfortable in their ritualistic traditions. They rejected
this strange good news.

After Jesus' death and resurrection, Luke recorded the
uprising in Ephesus. Paul's good news changed hearts, and
Demetrius, who produced silver shrines to the Greek goddess
Artemis, lost a large amount of business.

Who is your Demetrius, contented in traditions and rejecting
your good news?

O Lord, our God, give us the courage to continue sharing the
good tidings of great joy offered two thousand years ago.

Courage to Share the Good News of Jesus Christ

Jesus replied, "Don't be afraid! From now on you'll be fishing for the souls of men!"
LUKE 5:10 TLB

My friend makes peapod necklaces out of clay. Each pod contains five peas. Each pea is a different color. The first pea is gold, to symbolize God's holiness. Following in order are: black—the sinful world; red—the blood of Christ; white— forgiveness of sins; and finally, green—everlasting life.

During my annual medical exam, my doctor looked at my peapod and asked, "Is there a significance to your necklace?"

Wearing the peapod necklace opens the door often closed by people we don't know well. My friend carries a few with her to offer strangers during her daily errands. Her humble ministry emboldens me to seek ways to share because the Gospel must first be preached to all nations.

Heavenly Father, thank You for planting the idea of Peapod Gospels in my friend's heart. Please grant us the courage You have given her to share Your truth in unique ways. And may You continue to bless her and her work.

Courage to Deliver Bad News

And the servants of David were afraid
to tell him that the child was dead.
2 SAMUEL 12:18 NASB

No one wants to be the bearer of bad news. Are we more afraid of hurt feelings, or of their response? Will they quietly weep or tear the room apart in violent outrage?

Sometimes they surprise us, as David did his servants. David fasted and wept while his son was sick, praying that the child might live. When he learned his child had died, he got up and dressed. Knowing he would see his son in heaven, he was able to move forward. Psalm 112:7 states that a righteous man shall not be afraid of evil tidings. His heart is fixed, trusting in the Lord.

It's far more kind to deliver sad tidings quickly with gentleness than to wait for the right moment. There is no good time for bad news. We can remind them to fix their hearts in righteousness, trust in the Lord, and welcome His embrace.

Give us the courage and the right words, O God,
to bring comfort when delivering bad news.

Fear of Change

*Behold, I tell you a mystery: we shall
not all sleep, but we shall all be changed.*
1 CORINTHIANS 15:51 NKJV

Life-changing moments begin before our birth. We grow from a zygote to a baby in thirty-six weeks, developing muscular, skeletal, and nervous system; blood vessels; organs; and tiny fingers and toes. Change continues rapidly on this side of the womb, too. We learn to walk and talk, move from a liquid diet to solids, and grow in stature.

So why do some of us fear change? It often means letting go of our comfort zone and the familiar people, places, and things we've come to treasure. Yet our joy increases as we move forward in the newness of life.

While the world is in an uproar, we eagerly await the trumpet. Our light at the end of the tunnel will be Christ in His glory as He returns in the sky to take us with Him.

*Gracious Father, thank You for giving us hope in the
change to come. As we change from mortal to immortal,
we will be united with You to enjoy our heavenly home.*

Fear of Life's Ruts

Jesus Christ the same yesterday, and to day, and for ever.
HEBREWS 13:8 KJV

———

We take the same route to work every day, eat the same turkey sandwich for lunch, work on the same humdrum paperwork, and then take the same route home again. Our schedule has become a rut, and we begin to dread the sameness of our dull, drab lives. But we don't dare change anything that might affect our time line. That's when our fear of ruts becomes a phobia. We have the knowledge to mix up the schedule, but not the courage.

While our lives appear to be static, changes take place every day. The traffic flow to and from work changes, depending on light cycles. The bread slices have a different shape than the sandwich we ate the day before.

As we look at the sameness of life, we see hints of changes. That's because only one is unchanging—Jesus Christ, our eternal Savior.

Father in Heaven, when we get caught up in
our ruts of life, prompt us to make changes
that remind us of Your timeless love.

Fear of Relocating

"Have I not commanded you? Be strong and courageous!
Do not tremble or be dismayed, for the LORD
your God is with you wherever you go."

JOSHUA 1:9 NASB

After my grandfather's death, our dad sold the construction business they shared in Texas to move the family to Florida. He told our mom he'd always wanted to own and operate a motel in the tropics.

On a hot August morning, two anxious adults, three distressed youngsters, and a loquacious Siamese cat headed east in two cars. Trading tumbleweeds for palm trees didn't sit well with my brother, sister, and me.

Looking back now as an adult, I realize the courage my parents must've had to leave familiar surroundings and make that long trek into an unknown land. I see a similarity in our relocation and the Israelites' move into the land of promise. We had lost our grandfather; they had lost Moses. We made the long journey under God's protective hand. They crossed over the Jordan with His blessing.

Gracious God, You are with us wherever we go.
Let us be strong and courageous in every move.

Fear of Being Martha

But the Lord answered and said to her, "Martha, Martha,
you are worried and bothered about so many things."
LUKE 10:41 NASB

We invited the pastor and some friends to our home for supper. Preparing in the midst of constant interruptions, I frantically dusted furniture, vacuumed floors, and scoured bathrooms. I noticed the fan in the living room had cat hairs fluttering in the wind. As I headed toward it carrying a damp rag, one of my friends called.

She reassured me with calming words. Reminding me of Jesus' encounter with Martha and Mary, she said, "Everyone will be interested in what the pastor has to say. No one will notice if you forget to dust a knick-knack."

After dessert, my longhaired cat made her grand entrance into the room, flipping her tail like a feather boa. My friend laughed and pointed to the fan—yes, the fan I forgot to wipe down—and said, "Oh look. The fan has streamers blowing out that match the cat!"

Dear Lord, thank You for dissolving my fears with
a splash of humor, and for the blessing of friendship.

Fear of Competition

In a race everyone runs, but only one person
gets first prize. So run your race to win.
1 CORINTHIANS 9:24 TLB

Whether in business, politics, or sports, competition reveals to us—and to our rivals—how proficient or deficient we are at a specific talent. When we're pitted against one whose ability seems far superior to ours, self-doubt attempts to trample our confidence. We don't give up mentally before we get started physically. We need to compete to grow and improve.

Competition compels us to diligently focus on self-discipline. As Christians, our race isn't against other humans, but against the adversary. Every lap and every hurdle represent our quest to win souls for Christ. God gave each of us a special talent to use for His glory. Some have a ministry of music, acting, or artwork. Others preach or write. We might not win an earthly, perishable prize, but our gold medal is waiting in heaven as we trounce the competition.

God our Father, we won't slow down or stop until we've run
this race with endurance to win, and crossed Your finish line.

Fear of Making a Bad First Impression

Don't be selfish; don't live to make a good impression on others.
Be humble, thinking of others as better than yourself.
PHILIPPIANS 2:3 TLB

You only have one chance to make a good first impression.

A member of our church thought I was a snob when we first met. She mistook my shyness for snootiness. We later became good friends, but now I try to step out of my comfort zone and welcome newcomers.

My comfort zone, the pew we occupy every Sunday, became my comfy cocoon in the years we've sat on the third row to the left of the center aisle. Of course, I know the regulars who sit near us. But my fear of making a bad first impression kept me from greeting strangers.

Reading Philippians, I've learned an important lesson: it isn't about me.

When we put others first, we can't help but make a good first impression, not only for ourselves, but also for the Lord Jesus Christ, whom we represent in everything we do.

Gracious Lord, give us the courage
to step out of our comfy cocoons.

Fear of the Past

I have considered the days of old,
the years of ancient times.
PSALM 77:5 NKJV

We can't escape the past. Thoughts, words, and deeds we'd like to forget surface when we least expect them. Sad memories dredge up old pains. My husband's epilepsy-induced memory loss erased any recollection of a family wedding, but not tragic events that scarred his heart.

The Psalm of Asaph shows us how to face the past. He says, " 'But I will remember the years of the right hand of the Most High.' I will remember the works of the LORD; surely I will remember Your wonders of old" (Psalm 77:10–11 NKJV).

We can view the past as a gift from the Lord, for without it we wouldn't be who we are today. Joy comes in remembering what God has done for us.

When I agreed to write short stories for *Heavenly Humor for the Mother's Soul*, painful memories of my mother's suffering emerged. Then God reminded me of her happier, amusing moments. The dawn of joyful memories dispelled the darkness of my youth.

Lord, thank You for giving us the gift of the past.

Courage to Face the Future

"For I know the plans that I have for you,"
declares the LORD, "plans for welfare and not
for calamity to give you a future and a hope."
JEREMIAH 29:11 NASB

The future of our nation looks bleak. The moral compass is spinning, searching for the point of legitimacy buried in sin long ago. Our leaders call evil good, and good evil. Do we fret in despair, or carry on in prayer?

The godly men and women of thirteen colonies considered their future dismal, too. Yet with God's help, a mighty nation grew out of their bravery and sacrifice. They sowed the seeds of hope for future generations. If we plant the seeds of the Gospel of Jesus Christ, then those who follow us will find a harvest of hope.

Is our world falling apart, or falling into place? God knows the plans He has for us, for our nation, and the world. He tells us His plans in His Word.

Dear Lord, we've read the end of the Bible. Knowing Your
victory over evil encourages us to face our futures with hope.

Fear of Growing Up

When I became a man, I did away with childish things.
1 CORINTHIANS 13:11 NASB

The "Peter Pan Syndrome" describes men who fear living as mature adults. I didn't find a syndrome for women who suffer the same qualms. How often have I cried out, "I want my mommy!" when stress fills my world. I want to curl up in my mother's lap and let her stroke my hair and say, "Now, now. It'll be okay."

Adulthood means facing the Big, Scary R: Responsibility. Not only are we accountable for our own lives, but also for those dependent upon us.

Paul admonished the Corinthians to be mature in their faith and gave them the tools—his letters—to help. The Big, Scary R isn't so frightening when we accept the responsibility for our spiritual growth. As we mature in our faith, we find more joy in being adults. Sharing Bible truths with others of like mind helps us grow in our knowledge of God.

Father God, as we grow up in years and in Your Word,
we learn more about Your love for us. . .Your grown-up children.

Fear of Growing Old

Now Joshua was old, advanced in years. And the
LORD said to him: "You are old, advanced in years."
JOSHUA 13:1 NKJV

During our daily Bible reading, my husband stopped at Joshua 13:1. He sat back and said, "You know you're old when God says you're old."

I recall ushering in each year with hope. Then decades barged in, shouting like impatient children. The twenty-first century bulldozed through the contentment of my youth, dragging me behind it as I shouted, "Wait! Slow down!"

It didn't listen.

How swiftly the time has flown by. Having more yesterdays than tomorrows, my fears of growing old bring me to tears. I don't feel my age, until I need help getting up from a squatted position.

When my fear of growing old overwhelms me, I turn to God's Word. Proverbs 31 reminds me that He created me to be a woman of strength and dignity, to have no fear of old age.

Will I need God to tell me when I'm old?

Lord, grant me courage to grow old gracefully,
using the time I have left to share Your love.

Courage to Discard Something Old

"And who would use old wineskins to store new wine?"
MATTHEW 9:17 TLB

Old cars break down, old clothes wear out, and old wineskins lose their elasticity.

I trembled when I sold my old car. It served me well for seventeen years, despite my first-name relationship with several tow truck drivers. A similar angst came upon me when I had to throw away my old "Brownfield Cubs" sweatshirt. The fighting bear logo lost his fists in 1970.

Jesus' example of old wineskins pointed to another old item to be discarded: the limits of the old forms of the law. The new wine represents His new covenant—the new teaching of God's grace through Christ's sacrifice. His death, burial, and resurrection put an end to the necessity of the old sacrificial system.

Jesus came to fulfill the law, and in that fulfillment, ushered in a new and better way to worship our Father.

Heavenly Father, as we struggle to discard our old and no longer useful items, please help us to remember the early Jewish Christians who struggled with discarding their old belief system to embrace Christ.

Courage in a Season of Desperation

To You they cried out and were delivered;
in You they trusted and were not disappointed.

PSALM 22:5 NASB

A chaplain shared the account of his friend who served at the Pentagon during the attacks on September 11, 2001. Burns covered over sixty percent of the officer's body. His lungs filled with fluid, nearly drowning him. Deep within his soul, he cried out to the Lord, "Jesus, I'm coming to You."

He survived, not because of his bravery or expert training, but because Jesus heard his cries. In his season of desperation, he endured thirty-nine surgeries and skin grafts over forty percent of his body.

Desperation doesn't always strike and run. Sometimes it lingers for a season. The woman who touched Jesus' robe suffered twelve years of hopelessness. Adding to her anguish, her people ostracized her because of her prolonged uncleanness. Her mere touch of faith, brought immediate healing. Jesus called her "daughter." In trusting Him, she became a child of God.

Merciful God, in our season of desperation,
when only Jesus hears our screams, we trust
in You for deliverance from our distresses.

Courage to Take a Leap of Faith

For by You I can run against a troop,
by my God I can leap over a wall.
PSALM 18:29 NKJV

"Why would anyone jump out of a perfectly good airplane?" asked our friend, an army chaplain, who joined the 82nd Airborne Division.

With only three weeks of training, he had to jump out of a perfectly good airplane.

Aboard the aircraft, the solid red light meant, "Wait."

The green light flashed. The commander yelled, "Go!"

The chaplain ran through the open door to leap into the unknown. With the ground spiraling toward him, he counted to four, and the parachute automatically opened.

The chaplain's presence encouraged the soldiers. Wherever they went, he went. Whatever challenges they faced, he also endured. Isn't that also true of Christ? Jesus is with us when we must leap out of our comfort zones. When His green light flashes, we can bravely take His hand and go.

O God, our rock and our fortress, give us courage
to take Your hand when You flash the green light
that says, "Go." Help us take that leap in faith.

Courage to Trust the Lord

But the centurion said, "Lord, I am not worthy
for You to come under my roof, but just say
the word, and my servant will be healed."
MATTHEW 8:8 NASB

A centurion commanded a hundred Roman soldiers. They were zealous because they feared him more than the enemy.

Compassion, not fierceness, brought the centurion of Capernaum to Jesus. We can learn much from his brief encounter.

He approached the Lord with concern for his servant's well being. God wants us to love one another and look out for each other in this way.

He cited his own unworthiness. God's word tells us a man's pride will bring him low, but a humble spirit will obtain honor.

He trusted Jesus at His word. To say in prayer, "Just say the word," shows faith in God's heartfelt compassion when we don't see His hand working in our lives.

He acknowledged Jesus' divine authority. Just as God spoke the world into existence, Jesus can speak healing into a paralytic.

O God, whose Word I praise, send forth Your
lovingkindness and Your truth. Give us the courage
to trust you enough to pray, "Just say the word."

Courage to Live

"I went down to the moorings of the mountains; the earth with its bars closed behind me forever; yet You have brought up my life from the pit, O LORD, my God."
JONAH 2:6 NKJV

Our chaplain friend shared the statistics of suicide among soldiers returning from war. After valiantly serving this country, they come home with a sense of hopelessness. The bloodshed and suffering they witness is more than any human being's consciousness should have to bear.

Prayer hotlines hear countless stories from others who battle despair.

Jonah lost all hope when he ran away from God, but the Lord brought him out of the deep pit of depression. That's where we are when suicidal thoughts enter our minds—running away from God. Listen for that quiet voice that whispers, "I love you, My child. I will strengthen you and give you a life worth living because I live."

Loving Father, I lift up that soldier, police officer, teenager, parent, and others who are so filled with distress that they can't see You. Open their eyes with Your tender embrace. Give them the courage to live.

Fear of Separation

*For perhaps he was for this reason separated from you
for a while, that you would have him back forever.*

PHILEMON 1:15 NASB

Children grow up and leave for college or a career. Friends relocate for marriage or work. Death takes a spouse, a sibling, or a parent. Separation takes many forms. Most are difficult to accept, but nothing is worse than separation from God. Adam and Eve suffered that fate when, due to their rebellion, God expelled them from the presence of His love. We've been trying to find our way back since the fall. God provided the Way—Jesus.

Onesimus ran away as a slave, but returned as a brother in Christ. Paul petitioned Philemon to forgive Onesimus's defiance and offered to pay the debt the former slave owed.

Like Philemon's slave, we ran away from God, defiantly seeking our own way. Christ rescued us, paid the outstanding debt we owed, and returned us as coheirs to the kingdom.

*God our Father, circumstances separate us from
our loved ones, but nothing will separate us
from Your love through Christ Jesus.*

Fear of Isolation

My God, my God, why have You forsaken me?
PSALM 22:1 NASB

I turned on my tablet to begin the online biblical research for my writing project. An error message popped up on the screen stating I was off-line. I sighed. Another hindrance to my work. I sent a text message to my sister. It didn't go through. I called her. One ring, and it disconnected. I called a friend. The same thing happened. I tried to go online using my smartphone. The same error message popped up.

I considered asking my neighbors if they had phone service, but none of them were home. I had no contact with the outside world. The fear of isolation closed in on me. I fought back with prayer.

Jesus cried, "'ELI, ELI, LAMA SABACHTHANI?'" (Matthew 27:46 NASB). Bearing the sins of the world as He died on the cross isolated Him from the love of the Father. Since He loves me enough to suffer that for me, I can hold on to Him in my fear of isolation.

Dear God, knowing You are always with us,
we will never be isolated.

The Courage to Ask

Joseph of Arimathea came, a prominent member of the
Council, who himself was waiting for the kingdom of God;
and he gathered up courage and went in before Pilate,
and asked for the body of Jesus.

MARK 15:43 NASB

Abraham mustered the courage to ask God to spare Sodom and Gomorrah, bartering down to ten righteous people. The Lord answered each plea with a yes.

Joseph of Arimathea, fearful of his fellow Jews, had to gather up courage to request Jesus' body for burial.

Each man asked for favor that matched God's will. God would have spared Sodom and Gomorrah if only He had found ten righteous men there. Pilate unknowingly fulfilled the details of Jesus' burial foretold by the prophet Isaiah.

We have no need to fear asking anything of the Lord, if we ask it in Christ's name. For in His name is God's will. Jesus said, "'For everyone who asks receives, and he who seeks finds, and to him who knocks it will be opened'" (Matthew 7:8 NASB).

Gracious Father, thank You for allowing us to boldly
come to Your throne of glory with our petitions.

Courage to Be Appraised

If any man's work which he has built on it remains, he will receive a reward. If any man's work is burned up, he will suffer loss; but he himself will be saved, yet so as through fire.
1 CORINTHIANS 3:14–15 NASB

Fear of exams changes our study habits. Hoping for more than just a passing grade, we pay closer attention to the teacher, then read and reread the text until we're comfortable with the course material.

In the workforce, fear of job loss or no pay increase drives us to improve our professional behavior for an upcoming job evaluation. We make punctuality a priority, double-check our work, and put on a happy face for our coworkers and managers.

As God's people, we face a future heavenly appraisal. Not a judgment of condemnation, but of rewards. The decisions we make today will determine how well we fare before God's Bema Seat. Will we present Him with works of wood, hay, and straw—or gold, silver, and precious gems?

Merciful Father, keep us ever mindful of the impact our decisions today make on our eternity with You in heaven.

Courage to Be Strong

*"Behold, God is my salvation, I will trust and
not be afraid; For the Lord God is my strength
and song, and He has become my salvation."*

Isaiah 12:2 nasb

A local news station ran a story about a mother of two who works a full-time job, attends graduate school, and is training to compete in an international weight-lifting competition. Video of her squatting to lift the two-hundred-pound barbell ran in the background as the anchor explained her decision and what it entailed.

I watched in awe, wondering how she had the physical strength to lift those barbells, the stamina to keep up with her other responsibilities, and the emotional stability to maintain her work-family-leisure balance.

Maintaining a busy workday, then coming home to hausfrau duties is a struggle. I wouldn't attempt to lift a two-hundred-pound barbell. Getting a twenty-pound container of kitty litter from the car to the back door is more than I can manage sometimes. I pray for the Lord to carry me through each day.

And He always does.

God of my salvation, thank You for being my strength.

Courage to Face the Truth

"And you will know the truth,
and the truth will make you free."
JOHN 8:32 NASB

The truth hurts only if we don't want to hear it. If I have parsley stuck in my teeth, it isn't painful for someone to let me know. If a loved one is seriously ill, the truth of the diagnosis and treatment can hurt deeply. But knowing the truth opens doors and sets us free for more choices and opportunities.

The Jewish authorities Jesus spoke to did not want to hear His truth. They asserted their lineage to Abraham and, since they hadn't been enslaved, questioned His comment about being free. Their claim to be free from sin was nullified by their murderous thoughts toward Jesus.

God's truth hurts when we first give up a sinful lifestyle. The pain of surrendering our enslaved minds and hearts is soon replaced by the healing freedom in Christ Jesus. That new freedom gives us the courage to face the truth.

Righteous Father, thank You for giving us
freedom in the divine revelation of Your truth.

Courage to Say the Right Thing

Everyone enjoys giving good advice, and how wonderful
it is to be able to say the right thing at the right time!
PROVERBS 15:23 TLB

Our loved ones come to us for advice. The right thing to say might not be what they want to hear. If we hold back on our advice, heartache may ensue. If we go full force with our recommendations, the relationship might suffer. The first step is to pray for guidance.

We can take a cue from the One who always said the right thing at the right time. Jesus answered questions posed to Him with wise, thought-provoking questions, such as in Mark 10:17, when a man asked Him, "'Good Teacher, what shall I do to inherit eternal life?'" Jesus' first reply was, "'Why do you call Me good?'" (NASB). Did Jesus first want to establish that the man knew of His deity?

When we determine the real need, then we can offer the right advice with the courage to say the right thing at the right time.

Heavenly Father, remind us to look
to You before offering our advice.

Courage to Use Restraint

When there are many words, transgression is unavoidable,
but he who restrains his lips is wise.
PROVERBS 10:19 NASB

Jephthah's unrestrained vow cost him his beloved daughter. A better word choice would've produced a happier outcome as he came home from battle.

Many times we've feared the backlash of words spoken in zeal or anger. We can't pull them back in after they've been released. The consequences of our words can be far-reaching, affecting family and friends, and even strangers, for generations.

Jesus said to the Pharisees in Matthew 12:34, "'For the mouth speaks out of that which fills the heart'" (NASB). If fire dwells in the heart, then sparks will come out of the mouth. The urge to respond, rebuke, or retaliate is often stronger than our ability to hold the tongue. There is wisdom in a ten-second pause to take a deep breath. Fear of the repercussions of hasty words can give us the courage to use restraint.

Heavenly Father, since we shall give an accounting
for every careless word we speak, let our words
reflect calm hearts filled with the love of Christ.

Fear in the Garden

*And the L*ORD *God planted a garden eastward in Eden;*
and there he put the man whom he had formed.
GENESIS 2:8 KJV

I didn't inherit my grandmother's ability to grow fresh vegetables. How I miss her homegrown, home-canned black-eyed peas. Squash from her backyard made my mouth water.

After trying to grow roses, I accepted the fact that my black thumb limited my gardening skills to sticking waterproof, artificial plants into a flowerpot. Even an herb garden in my kitchen window died from either too much or not enough water. Plants tremble in fear in my presence.

How glorious God's garden must have been! Fresh fruit and vegetables abounded, with every kind of flower and tree to bring a tapestry of colors and fresh fragrances.

Since I fail at growing flowers, fruits, and vegetables, there is another way to plant for the Lord. An impromptu smile, an act of kindness, and soothing words will bloom fearlessly in my garden of the Gospel of Jesus Christ. And my black thumb won't affect it at all.

Gracious God, let all I do bring glory to You.

Fear of Falling

The Lord sustains all who fall and
raises up all who are bowed down.
PSALM 145:14 NASB

My foot slipped in something squishy on the top step of my porch. I tumbled down, slamming my shin against the two lower steps. A trip to the emergency room confirmed no broken bones. I had to stay off my bruised leg for the next few days.

In fear, I avoided using those steps after that treacherous fall. I gathered my courage a few months later and tried to climb up them to the porch. I stumbled, landed on my knee, and put my hand through the screen door. As I cradled my skinned knee with my injured hand, I said, "Might as well pray while I'm down here."

That statement is also true when I stumble in my faith. When I lose my biblical balance, I trip over my Christian duty to love others. Praying on my knees restores my equilibrium and curbs my fear of falling.

Dear Lord, thank You for sustaining me when I
fall and lifting me up when I bow to You in prayer.

Fear of Sudden Noises

*For the Lord Himself will descend from heaven with
a shout, with the voice of an archangel, and with the
trumpet of God. And the dead in Christ will rise first.*

1 Thessalonians 4:16 nkjv

A bang explodes outside. Is it a gun, or a car's backfire? An alarm shrieks without warning. Are we in danger, or are technicians testing it? Glass shatters in the middle of the night. Is it a burglar, or has the cat knocked over a priceless vase? A thunderclap rattles the windows. Is it a storm coming our way, or an F-16 soaring over the house? Shouting voices roar from the street. Is it an angry mob, or a parade for a returning hero?

Sudden, loud noises of any kind can make us jump out of our skin. But there is one sound we all look forward to—that of the Lord's shout and trumpet blast just before we rise to meet Him in the air.

*Almighty God, when sudden noises frighten us,
help us to remember Your promise that You
will come for us in the twinkling of an eye.*

Fear of Public Speaking

Then Moses said to the Lord, "O my Lord, I am not
eloquent, neither before nor since You have spoken to
Your servant; but I am slow of speech and slow of tongue."
Exodus 4:10 NKJV

As a shy adolescent, giving a book report brought on a stuttering fear. Simple words evaporated. The phrase, "He forgot," became "He. . .stopped knowing." My undiagnosed dyspraxia also complicated matters. My brain jumbled my words.

I read about Moses' first encounter with God and wondered if he got his words mixed, too.

Forty years of living in Egypt should have equipped Moses to speak before Pharaoh. Did he really have a speech impediment, or did fear of his enemy tie his tongue?

God said He would teach Moses what to say. Taking my cue from His promise in Exodus, I followed the Lord's leading to drama classes. He vanquished my fear of public speaking through a stage play.

Knowing God provides our words gave me courage to publicly speak about the Lord Christ Jesus.

Gracious Lord, we pray for the courage to speak
openly about Your love through our Savior.

Fear of Outcomes

*We can make our plans, but the
final outcome is in God's hands.*
PROVERBS 16:1 TLB

The most famous upset in American voting history was the 1948 presidential election. Every prediction indicated the incumbent, President Harry Truman, would lose to New York Governor Thomas Dewey. The *Chicago Daily Tribune* editors were so sure of the outcome, they printed an errant headline in advance.

Satan used Judas in his attempt to thwart God's plan for our salvation. His scheme backfired on him, but benefited those of us who believe in Jesus' sacrifice on the cross to pay for our sin.

The apostle Paul planned to go to Bithynia to preach the Word, but the Spirit of Jesus sent him to Macedonia instead. The outcome saved Paul from possible harm and brought the Gospel to Europe.

When making plans, we might fear the outcome because of unforeseen consequences. Will they backfire on us, like the 1948 election headline, or bring unexpected benefits, like Paul's journey to Macedonia? Give that fear to God. It's in His hands.

*Almighty God, we find courage knowing
we can trust You in all outcomes.*

Fear of the News Media

*Sing to the LORD, bless His name; proclaim good
tidings of His salvation from day to day.*
PSALM 96:2 NASB

In a conversation I overheard the other day, a woman told her
companions she was afraid to watch the news. She claimed,
"It's scary, it's biased, and worse yet, it's all lies."

I remember when journalists reported cheerful stories, hid
their political leanings, and their articles had to be truthful.
Some anchormen and anchorwomen freely offered hopeful
comments that represented their faith in the Lord.

News affiliates now seem afraid to give God the glory for
any good news. They don't encourage falling to our knees in
prayer during tragedies, lest anti-Christian groups file a lawsuit.

Since their tongues are tied with an invisible gag, it is up
to us to sing to the Lord and bless His name. We have the
ability—if not the responsibility—to proclaim His good tidings
of salvation anytime a reporter sticks a microphone or camera
in front of us.

*Dear Lord, please give us the courage to reveal
Your truth anytime we have a news audience.*

Courage to Pray Openly

"But you, when you pray, go into your room, and when you have shut your door, pray to your Father who is in the secret place; and your Father who sees in secret will reward you openly."
MATTHEW 6:6 NKJV

I read a story, true or not I'm unsure, about a family in a restaurant who quietly prayed over the food after their waiter served the meal. When they received their check, the waiter had given them a twenty percent discount because he appreciated their courage to pray openly.

Jesus teaches that our prayer time should be quiet and in secret. The Lord hears our prayers, even when we can't speak. He knows what is on our hearts before we ask. Coming to Him with our petitions and thanks, even in public, shows we depend on Him for everything.

A family joining hands in a restaurant sets an example for other Christians. Let our bowed heads and soft prayers provide a public witness of our faith.

*Dear Lord, give us the courage to pray
in public as we would in private.*

Courage to Take in Strays

*And Jesus answering said, "Were there not
ten cleansed? But where are the nine?"*
LUKE 17:17 KJV

A stray black cat befriended my husband. With two indoor-only cats, we couldn't bring him inside.

We put "Blackie" in the laundry room, fed him, and saw to his needs, then posted "lost pet" signs. My husband sat on the laundry room floor every evening, comforting the stray. A week later, his owner called. He lived a block away.

My husband's concern for strays wasn't limited to cats. He offered help to five distressed men. One suffered from mental illness, another had family disputes, and three were divorced. We fed them, listened to their woes, and offered words of comfort. Of the five, only two remained friends.

What about the other three? Even "Blackie" returned to say thanks.

When only one leper returned to praise Jesus for the miraculous healing, the Lord didn't "un-heal" the other nine.

Our motive for fostering injured souls isn't to garner gratitude, but to convey Christ's love.

*Thank You, Lord, for the courage to take in stray
cats and men to share Your lovingkindness.*

Fear of Asking Forgiveness

If we confess our sins, He is faithful and just to forgive us our sins and to cleanse us from all unrighteousness.
1 John 1:9 nkjv

I broke my online rule and responded to an email in anger. I inadvertently clicked the "reply all" button. One of the addressees belonged to a member of a Bible study I attended. How could I face her? I considered dropping out of the study, but instead prayed for the courage to approach her and a moment alone to ask her forgiveness.

Our next study met at a restaurant. As we took our seats around the table, she sat next to me. Each of the ladies left us—one to get napkins, another to get water, another to check the desserts. I saw my answered prayer as we sat alone at the table. When I offered my heartfelt apology, she looked at me wide-eyed.

"Really? I don't remember that." She smiled and added, "Whatever you said, of course I forgive you."

Forgiving Lord, thank You for giving me the courage, the moment, and place to ask and receive forgiveness.

Courage to Forgive

Jesus said to him, "I do not say to you,
up to seven times, but up to seventy times seven."
MATTHEW 18:22 NASB

My husband's career as a Realtor allowed him the time to join a men's monthly luncheon and Bible study.

One of the men decided to move out of state. Rather than list his home with my husband, he gave his business to a nonbeliever.

My husband forgave him, while I stewed in anger. How could that man so blatantly disrespect a fellow Christian?

He had the audacity to send us a postcard after he moved. Months later, another card arrived. More followed every few months.

My heart grumbled with each one. Then I realized the postcards were the Lord's reminders to forgive him. Sometimes forgiveness is a process, especially when the wrong was committed against a loved one.

We still receive postcards at least twice a year. I rebuke the tinge of anger when it surfaces. God forgave him. I can too.

Dear God, give us the courage to rebuke our
unforgiving attitudes and show Your unfailing love.

Fear of Being Falsely Accused

*Do what is right; then if men speak against you, calling you
evil names, they will become ashamed of themselves for
falsely accusing you when you have only done what is good.*
1 PETER 3:16 TLB

Joseph didn't complain as he endured prison after a false
accusation. The Lord had already planned to put him in charge
under Pharaoh in order to preserve the Israelites. Joseph fulfilled
God's objective.

Paul and Silas, accused of inciting a riot, were beaten and
jailed. An earthquake proved their faithfulness, bringing the
jailer and his family to faith in the risen Christ. They fulfilled
God's objective.

A false accusation could be as simple as a mistaken identity
or as serious as a heinous crime. Would we have the courage
to seek the Lord's plan in the harsh experience? He has a great
purpose for each of us. Like Joseph, Paul, and Silas, let us fulfill
God's objective.

*Almighty God, when others hurl false accusations
at us, give us courage to endure it as we
await the fulfillment of Your objective.*

Fear of Miracles

*Then fear came upon every soul, and many wonders
and signs were done through the apostles.*
ACTS 2:43 NKJV

A miracle is an extraordinary event that signifies God's presence in our human existence.

The Lord gave His apostles authority to perform signs and wonders. These miracles helped the early church grow under Peter's leadership.

Although miracles have occurred throughout history, many people still deny or fear them. They don't believe a miracle occurred, but merely a coincidence. Others argue the authority to perform miracles didn't extend beyond the apostles. Some fear seeking a miracle would take their eyes off the Lord.

Did a coincidence save survivors of an airplane crash? Where did the man who prayed over a child hit by a car get his authority to do so? Did the healing of a terminal illness sidetrack the former patient's focus on God?

Whether we witness a worldwide phenomenon or the everyday miracle of a blooming sunflower, let us utilize God's signs and wonders to lead others to Him.

*Almighty God, thank You for miracles. We praise
You for the wondrous signs that point us to You.*

Courage to Ask for Help

You drew near when I called on You; You said, "Do not fear!"
LAMENTATIONS 3:57 NASB

My work as a legal secretary leaves me drained at the end of each day. An approaching deadline adds stress to my part-time work as a writer. Monitoring my husband's medications and doctor appointments makes my head spin. I have neither the time nor energy to clean the house.

I was afraid to seek help from anyone, especially the Lord. Asking meant I'd have to relinquish my Super Woman cape. Then one day, in a puddle of tears, I cried out to God.

He reminded me of my blessings: pleasant coworkers in the law office, writer friends offering support and prayers, and the main blessing of my husband's slow, but sure, progress. Most days, he's strong enough to have supper ready when I get home from work.

Before I could ask for the Lord's help, I had to recognize what He had already done for me.

You have heard my voice, O God, and have not hidden Your ear from my prayer for relief. But replaced my fear with blessings.

Fear of Oncoming Pain

*The cords of death encompassed me and the terrors
of Sheol came upon me; I found distress and sorrow.*
PSALM 116:3 NASB

The familiar base-of-my-skull throbbing, the sign of another impending assault of cluster headaches, brought immobilizing panic.

The pain made my senses intensify to acute stages. The darkest room was too bright. Favorite foods nauseated me. My cats' tiptoeing on the carpet sounded like buffalo herds stampeding across the prairie. Each brutal episode lasted about three months.

The twenty-five medical specialists I consulted couldn't locate the pain's source. I had to lean on the Lord. I prayed fervently for relief, even for death. Members of my church prayed for healing. The pain gradually faded. . .until the next occurrence.

A retired upper-cervical specialist in my Sunday school class recognized the symptoms: my top vertebra was misaligned. After years of suffering and praying, the Lord provided relief from my distress and misery.

Thank You, God, for answering my prayers in Your time. Those headaches taught me to rely solely on You. Let others who call on Your name find relief from their fear of oncoming pain.

Courage to Kick an Unhealthy Habit

*Or do you not know that your body is a temple
of the Holy Spirit who is in you, whom you have
from God, and that you are not your own?*
1 Corinthians 6:19 NASB

As a teenager, I blamed my parents' divorce when I started to smoke. I struggled to give it up in my twenties.

Ten years later, I lit up again, blaming the stress of my cross-country move. A bout with pneumonia helped me quit.

Being cigarette-free for five years came to an end when I lost my job due to a back injury. My chiropractor offered to write off the remainder of my bill if I would quit smoking. A monetary incentive is a powerful ally—along with prayer.

I was convicted and reminded that my body belongs to God. He has granted me temporary housing during my mortal life. The only rent He demands is maintenance and tidiness.

I prayed, and God cast out any desire I had to smoke again. He is more powerful than our unhealthy habits.

*Heavenly Father, thank You for helping
us cleanse our temples and keep them tidy.*

Fear of the Appearance of Idleness

*And he said to them, "Why have you
been standing here idle all day long?"*
MATTHEW 20:6 NASB

"Idle hands are the devil's workshop," my dad used to say. "Trouble comes when we have nothing to do." He was a man of few idle moments, always working on a project and expecting me to help him.

The Bible says to avoid even the appearance of sin. But the appearance of idleness is more fearful since idleness can lead to the appearance of sin.

As a writer, I sometimes stand in the kitchen, staring out the window. That isn't idleness; it's work. I'm mentally chewing up words or creating a scene in my mind. Most of the time, though, I'm praying for inspiration.

When disease invaded my husband's body, he feared his fatigue made him appear lazy. He apologized every day for his lack of accomplishments, but he had no choice. Sapped strength won't budge.

We both feared what others thought of our idle appearance, but we don't have to fear God's opinion. He knows our circumstances.

Lord, let our idleness be filled with You.

Courage to Seek Opportunities to Do Good

As we have therefore opportunity, let us do good unto all men,
especially unto them who are of the household of faith.
GALATIANS 6:10 KJV

As a Realtor, my husband went above and beyond the expected services to his clients. When he listed an elderly woman's home for sale, a buyer suggested he lower the price because of repair issues. Having worked his way through college in construction, my husband had the knowledge and ability to fix the problems so she could get the full price. The thought of charging her for his work didn't enter his mind.

My natural shyness made it difficult for me to help others like my husband did. But his influence encouraged me to seek ways to reach out in kindness. In my service, I discovered that we couldn't out-give God. The more we help others, the more He sends others to help us. Every new opportunity lets us edify other believers, and those who have yet to accept Christ marvel at the love we show one another.

Father God, thank You for the blessings
of perpetual Christian service.

Courage to Not Compromise

If a godly man compromises with the wicked, it is
like polluting a fountain or muddying a spring.
PROVERBS 25:26 TLB

A compromise is a promise with concessions. We promise to give up ground on a transaction in exchange for a favorable position. Negotiation in real estate is a common practice and usually works well for both parties. However, yielding ground in defense of our faith obscures the clear Gospel of Jesus Christ.

Acquaintances offered their assistance during a difficult time, but they overshot the boundaries of helpfulness. God gave me the courage to submit a gracious, yet firm response. Although they meant well, I would not compromise my principles.

Abraham had the courage to not compromise when he took Isaac, his son—his only son—to offer as a sacrifice to the Lord. God honored Abraham's unfailing obedience and provided a substitution.

God will honor our faithfulness to Him, as He did Abraham, when we trust Him for the conclusion. Let Him provide the uncompromised alternative.

Gracious God, grant us the courage to not pollute the
fountain of faith with which You have cleansed our hearts.

Courage to Stay the Course

And the Lord shall deliver me from every evil work,
and will preserve me unto his heavenly kingdom:
to whom be glory for ever and ever. Amen.
2 TIMOTHY 4:18 KJV

Understanding the time we live in makes determining what to do more confusing. In Paul's charge to Timothy—and to us—we are supposed to preach the Word of God in an instant. Not only with our words, but with our actions, too.

We can reprove, rebuke, and exhort even when those we'll share the Gospel with don't want to follow sound doctrine. They would rather listen to ear-tickling stories than hear that Jesus died for their sins.

Paul started his good fight on the road to Damascus and ended with his death. Our good fight began the moment we accepted Christ as our Savior. With Him at our side, we will be watchful, patient, and bear unknown afflictions as we stay the course for the sake of the Gospel.

Glorious Father, stand with us and strengthen us
so that we can be Your vessels to deliver Your truth.

Courage to Break Man's Law to Obey God

"Let it be known to you, O king,
that we are not going to serve your gods or
worship the golden image that you have set up."
DANIEL 3:18 NASB

Shadrach, Meshach, and Abednego believed that God would deliver them from Nebuchadnezzar's hand, even if deliverance meant death in the fiery furnace.

It is illegal to openly worship Jesus in some countries. Even courts in the U.S. have drawn a faint line in the sand, obscuring the language of our Constitution. Our freedom of speech is violated when we are denied the right to pray in Christ's name or share our love for Him in public. Jesus warned that we would be hated because of His name. Litigious unbelievers bring lawsuits against us, and courts subject us to heavy fines for adhering to our Christian faith.

Our reward for trusting in God will surpass any penalty the courts may impose on us.

Father God, give us the courage to break man's law
when it's necessary to obey Your laws. Let us rejoice
and be glad, for our rewards in heaven are great.

Courage in Prison

And most of the brethren in the Lord,
having become confident by my chains,
are much more bold to speak the word without fear.
PHILIPPIANS 1:14 NKJV

Due to a tragic, fatal accident, our friend must serve many years in the state prison. Turning his prison cell into a mission field, he boldly seeks opportunities to tell inmates and correctional officers about Jesus.

In Philippi, Paul and Silas suffered brutal beatings for casting a spirit out of a slave girl. Then they were thrown into the deepest part of the prison, with their feet fastened in stocks. In spite of their severe wounds, they shared prayers and sang hymns of praise to God. Their actions brought many to a saving faith in Jesus Christ.

Like Paul, our friend knows his faith will point to the Lord. When others witness his joy in spite of his imprisonment, they become curious.

The Lord will use every tragedy to further His kingdom.

God our Father, please bless our friend with
the courage, the wisdom, and the words to
show Christ's love to others in his midst.

Fear of Injustice

*"Be very much afraid to give any other decision than
what God tells you. For there must be no injustice
among God's judges, no partiality, no taking of bribes."*
2 Chronicles 19:7 TLB

Judges aren't allowed to counsel with Almighty God, although
they should.

Moved by compassion for a repeat criminal begging for
another chance, a judge could impose a lighter sentence. That
same judge might throw the book at a first-time offender,
ignorant of judicial procedures.

At times, they render unmerited verdicts because of their
own biases. The guilty go free, and the innocent are jailed,
depending on the attorneys' legal knowledge and persuasiveness
with the court.

The duty of Supreme Court Justices calls for them to base
their opinions on the facts presented. But they can bring their
own preconceived attitudes to the bench. It's possible they'll
follow the prevailing wind, especially in high profile, media-
blitzed cases.

Like us, they're flawed human beings in need of the Lord.

*Dear God, help us to replace our fear of injustice
with prayers for our judges, elected and appointed.
Give them courage to consult You for their decisions.*

Courage to Demand Justice

The exercise of justice is joy for the righteous,
but is terror to the workers of iniquity.
PROVERBS 21:15 NASB

During a presidential election several years ago, a small group of volunteers made a distressing discovery. The supervisor of elections had denied all mail-in votes for our military personnel who served overseas. She claimed the ballots arrived too late to be counted, although the postmark indicated they were shipped well within the allowed timeframe.

The Bible tells us the Lord loves justice and does not forsake His godly ones. We prayed for courage to oppose a local government authority.

Our protests garnered media publicity. More people became aware of our grievance. The demands for justice flowed into the elections office like a raging river. Finally, the supervisor conceded and reversed the decision.

Our soldiers face fierce enemies every day to protect our right to vote. It was only fitting for us to fight a bureaucracy to protect their right to vote.

Gracious Lord, thank You for giving meek people a courageous
voice to demand justice for our men and women in uniform.

Fear of Being Caught Doing Wrong

Nathan then said to David, "You are the man!"
2 Samuel 12:7 NASB

When King David's efforts to conceal his treachery failed, he compounded his sin of adultery with murder.

Nathan's story of a poor man's ewe lamb opened David's eyes to the extent of his crimes.

David received the rebuke with a contrite heart and confessed his sin against the Lord. His selfish acts slandered God's good name.

Although God forgave David, the far-reaching consequences of his sin remained. The child conceived in adultery would die, and David's kingdom would come to ruin. Severe offenses call for serious punishment.

How often have we tried to hide evidence of our wrongs? Do we need a Nathan to give us a glimpse into our own hearts?

God is omniscient. He sees directly into our hearts. Repentance means agreeing with the Lord about our sin. While we are forgiven through Christ, the consequences of our actions must be addressed.

Father in heaven, whether caught or not,
please give us the courage to confess our sins
and the strength to endure the consequences.

Courage to Admit We're Wrong

Then David said to Nathan, "I have sinned against the Lord."
2 SAMUEL 12:13 NIV

The Lord sent the prophet Nathan to confront David about his sin. Nathan gave David an introspective scrutiny into his own heart.

David's crimes, though committed in secret, had to be judged publicly. God said he had "'given occasion to the enemies of the Lord to blaspheme'" (2 Samuel 12:14 NASB). He confessed his transgression against the Lord.

Admitting our guilt takes courage, especially when faced with the repercussions. It's tempting to pervert God's Word to justify our behavior or blame someone else. Our immediate confession will always be met with God's grace. The consequences of our bad behavior, however, cannot be averted. Like David, we've damaged God's name, and like David, we will see God's grace when we confess our sin to Him. For, "He is faithful and righteous to forgive us our sins and to cleanse us from all unrighteousness" (1 John 1:9 NASB).

Gracious Father, Your forgiveness will bring comfort,
and Your mercy will grant us courage to admit
we're wrong and confess our sins.

Fear of Doing Right

Now I pray to God that you do no evil, not that we should appear approved, but that you should do what is honorable, though we may seem disqualified.
2 CORINTHIANS 13:7 NKJV

A friend provided a refuge for some homeless people.

Acting on a tip from an undisclosed source, the local news media publicly attacked him. They alleged he exploited the poor because of the location of the temporary housing.

He realized he was theoretically wrong because of an antiquated land-use violation. Rather than fuel the media fire by responding in fear or panic, he quietly resigned from his elected post, as well as the various boards on which he served.

His anonymous accuser cost our city a great resource, and the families went back to the streets. But he continues to help others in need.

We may have the best intentions, but others' agendas or motives can hinder our honorable acts. As we seek opportunities to do right, let us examine every factor that could impede our efforts.

Merciful God, please guide us to overcome obstacles that hinder our achievement of Your work.

Fear of Guilt

And their sins and iniquities
will I remember no more.
HEBREWS 10:17 KJV

We've accepted Christ's gift of redemption for our sins. All our wicked acts—past, present, and future—are buried at the foot of Jesus' cross. Yet guilt creeps back into our minds, bringing with it the darkness of remorse. We linger on them, like a cow chewing her cud, trying to grind away the shame.

Those dreadful thoughts are not from the Holy Spirit, but from the adversary. Satan's accusing finger constantly pokes at us, jabbing us right in the heart, prodding us to doubt and fear.

God has forgiven our sins and remembers them no more. What logical reason do we have to focus on them?

When the devil attempts to strike fear in us with memories of our dastardly deeds, our best defense is to turn them into praises to God.

Merciful Father, You have cleansed us of the terrible
acts we have done, continue to do, and will do in
the future. Thank You for Your loving mercy and
willingness to forgive and forget our guiltiness.

Courage Against Slander

A perverse man spreads strife,
and a slanderer separates intimate friends.
PROVERBS 16:28 NASB

After an ugly divorce, a friend's ex-husband told their mutual acquaintances stories of her insane rants and abuse of their two sons. The rumors spread like a flu virus.

Instead of offering a defense or rebuttal to his slander, she quietly prayed for the Lord to shed light on the truth about her. She sat alone at her sons' sporting events as those who believed her husband's lies stood aloof. Week after week, they witnessed the loving support she gave the boys. Eventually, her calm demeanor and forgiving spirit proved him wrong. God had answered her prayers.

David's enemies fueled Saul's unfounded jealousy with their malicious slander. God answered his prayers and protected him from harm.

My friend's situation would have worsened had she responded in kind to her ex-husband's lies. She took the higher road by placing her reputation in the Lord's hands.

Father God, give us courage to trust in You when
others slander us out of jealousy or hatred.
Let us not retaliate, but respond in love.

Fear of Discipline

All discipline for the moment seems not to be joyful,
but sorrowful; yet to those who have been trained by it,
afterwards it yields the peaceful fruit of righteousness.
HEBREWS 12:11 NASB

Driving to our destination, flashing red and blue lights appeared in the rearview mirror. We were speeding, or we rolled through a stop sign. Perhaps a skid through a traffic light as it turned from yellow to red caught the officer's attention. I've never known a police officer to stop a driver just to say howdy.

There is no joy in a citation's fine, and the depletion of personal funds to pay it brings much sorrow. But joy comes later in a lesson hopefully learned.

Delayed joy is the same reason God disciplines us. He reproves us like a loving parent when we step out of line. Learning to obey Him prepares us to share His holiness. As He teaches us to live for Him through discipline, we learn to yield the fruit of righteousness.

Father God, grant us the gift of fearing discipline, which will
teach us to surrender our will to Yours in obedience.

Courage to Be Free

For you were called to freedom, brethren;
only do not turn your freedom into an opportunity
for the flesh, but through love serve one another.
GALATIANS 5:13 NASB

Freedom isn't free.

World history proves that too much freedom can be fatal. It leads to apathy, which leads to anarchy, which leads to slavery, which leads to destruction of our liberty.

God created us with a basic need to be free. Adam enjoyed freedom until he rebelled against his Creator. His apathy toward Eve made her vulnerable to the serpent. Adam and Eve became anarchists when Eve blamed the serpent, and Adam blamed God. Their choices enslaved them to Satan.

Jesus set us free from the slavery of sin. We must remain diligent not to slip back into the shackles of our base desires, diminishing the significance of Christ's ultimate sacrifice. Our earthly lusts are fed by selfishness. Offering our service in Christian love keeps our focus off ourselves and on the Lord.

O God our Creator, we praise You for giving us the courage
to keep the freedom Christ's death on the cross provided.

Courage to Vote

"Moreover you shall select from all the people able men,
such as fear God, men of truth, hating covetousness;
and place such over them to be rulers of thousands,
rulers of hundreds, rulers of fifties, and rulers of tens."

EXODUS 18:21 NKJV

Hidden in God's instructions to Moses for selecting righteous leaders is an organizational pyramid.

This shape reflects our elective process. The base, or bottom of the pyramid, signifies our national offices—rulers of thousands.

Above that is our regional level—rulers of hundreds.

Next up is our state level—rulers of fifties.

The apex, our local offices, is the most important level—rulers of tens. Local elections are far more effective because, at this stage, we control who reaches the descending levels. We can defeat or promote a candidate at the city or county elections, even by one vote.

Considering our local elections as a top-down process might give us the needed courage to exercise our moral obligation and vote—every time.

Father God, we pray for courage to select men and
women who are eager to serve according to Your will.

Courage to Seek Public Office

"Do not be called leaders; for One is your Leader, that is, Christ. But the greatest among you shall be your servant."
MATTHEW 23:10–11 NASB

Throwing her hat in the ring painted a target on my friend's back. She knew her opponents would clean out her closets in search of skeletons. They dredged through newspapers and court records, but found nothing to disparage her. So they fabricated a rumor. She won in spite of their mudslinging and served us well.

God decides who will serve the people. "He also chose David His servant and took him from the sheepfolds" (Psalm 78:70 NASB). The Israelites selected Saul as their king because of his handsome appearance. But God chose David, a young shepherd boy, because of his faithfulness.

The greatest elected officials in US history have been those with servants' hearts. They resisted the temptation to be leaders and sought the Lord's guidance in their decisions.

Holy God, You alone can turn a shepherd boy into a king. Give us courage to seek public office, win or lose, that we may learn to be Your servants in the process.

Courage to Resist Temptation

For since He Himself was tempted in that which He has suffered, He is able to come to the aid of those who are tempted.

<small>HEBREWS 2:18 NASB</small>

We often find food to be shared in the snack room where I work. One morning, a plate of assorted cheesecakes called to me as I walked in to put my lunch in the refrigerator.

After pouring coffee into my mug, I looked longingly at the chocolate swirl slice. I prayed a quick prayer, "Lead me not into temptation," and then scurried away to my workspace.

Temptation doesn't only come in the form of food. A TV program can entice us to watch one more episode instead of reading our Bibles. A warm blanket on a cold Sunday morning might persuade us to stay in bed instead of attending church. Old habits try to weaken our resolve.

Jesus, who endured temptation, is always here to help us in our weaknesses. All we have to do is pray and ask.

Our faithful Father God, thank You for providing us courage through Jesus Christ when we're faced with temptation.

Fear of Government

"You shall surely set a king over you
whom the LORD your God chooses."
DEUTERONOMY 17:15 NASB

Thomas Jefferson wisely said, "When the people fear the government, there is tyranny. When the government fears the people, there is liberty." He understood that a critical role of our government was to listen to the people.

At the adjournment of the Constitutional Convention in 1787, a woman asked Benjamin Franklin, "Well, Doctor, what have we got, a republic or a monarchy?"

Mr. Franklin answered, "A republic, if you can keep it."

Those prudent delegates used Deuteronomy 17:14–20 as guidance for creating our Constitution, emphasizing God-ordained restrictions on elected leaders.

Our three-pronged republic is comparable to a three-legged stool. If one leg grows too long, the stool topples. Fearful tyranny creeps in.

More than two hundred years later, ignorance and corruption have weakened the foundations of that biblical example. God's Word teaches that the only incorruptible government will be during the thousand-year reign of Christ. Until He returns, we look to God for courage.

Come quickly, Lord!

Gracious Father, You guided our founding fathers.
Please direct our leaders back to You.

Courage to Challenge Corrupt Leaders

Do not be deceived: "Evil company corrupts good habits."
1 CORINTHIANS 15:33 NKJV

We elect candidates to public office hoping they'll represent our views and the needs of our communities. Some of these men and women have the ability to remain true to the standards with which we've entrusted them. Others fall into the trap of "absolute power corrupts absolutely," as Lord Acton put it.

Did these elected officials succumb to a latent weakness of principles, or did they hide their flaws so well during their campaign that we missed them?

Instead of throwing our hands in the air, we have choices. We can publicly challenge their decisions, demand accountability from them, impeach them, or vote them out of office. We have a strong voice in the ballot box.

The apostle Paul reminds us that we are all imperfect people, so let us be conscientious in our duties to search for replacement candidates. We don't want to fall into the corruption trap ourselves.

Holy God, You blessed us with the blood-borne liberty
to elect our public servants. Please give us wisdom
and courage to hold them accountable or replace them.

Fearlessly Standing for Truth

"Be fearless in your stand for truth and honesty. And may God use you to defend the innocent," was his final word to them.

2 CHRONICLES 19:11 TLB

King Jehoshaphat admonished his God-appointed judges that there must be no injustice, nor partiality, nor taking of bribes. They were to seek the Lord's wisdom when rendering their judgments, and above all, to defend the innocent.

Taking a stand for God's truth and protecting the innocent must go hand-in-hand, especially today. Are unborn babies not the most innocent? Yet some are targeted for a horrible death. Society vilifies us because we work to rescue them.

Proponents of pregnancy termination call the child a fetus. That term means "little one," not "blob of lifeless flesh." All children, whether planned or unplanned, are a gift from the Lord.

As believers in Jesus Christ, His enemies are our enemies. We can't cave to worldly influence, but must bravely push back with the power of God.

O Holy God, let us draw upon Your strength and courage
to stand fearlessly for Your truth and honesty,
and defend our beloved, innocent babies.

Courage in Defeat

And it came to pass, when Moses held up his hand, that Israel prevailed: and when he let down his hand, Amalek prevailed.
Exodus 17:11 KJV

Where there is victory, there is also a defeat. It is an outcome for every challenge, whether in battle, a sporting event, or the workplace.

So many struggles we face weigh us down. Using our own strength, we grow weaker and weaker until defeat overcomes us.

In the battle against Amalek, Moses grew weary from holding up the staff of God. Aaron and Hur provided a stone for him to sit. They stood on either side of him, bolstering up his arms.

God could have held up the staff, relieving Moses of the responsibility of Joshua's fate. But He wanted to show us the importance of solidarity. Moses needed the help of his brother and brother-in-law.

As a team, we pull together and strengthen each other, even in the midst of defeat. Unaided, we face it alone.

Almighty God, give us the strength to support others facing trials, and the courage to ask for help in our own struggles.

Courage to Not Envy Others

Do not let your heart envy sinners,
but live in the fear of the LORD always.
PROVERBS 23:17 NASB

Envy is a green-eyed monster. It creeps in as admiration for something someone else has. Then, if we allow, that admiration grows until we desire to have the item for ourselves. It's out of our reach. Not affordable or practical, but we still desire it. Then the green-eyed monster develops into full-blown covetousness. That's when we want someone else's property so much that we'll take it by force. Nothing good comes from envy.

We might not know how the other person acquired the item we desire. Was it by theft or coercion from their own covetousness? Or was it a gift from the Lord for righteous living?

The sin of envy spits in God's eye. It says to Him, "You haven't given me enough. I want what others have."

In prayer, we can turn away the green-eyed monster before it lures us away from trusting God.

Lord, let us be content in what You have provided.
We know You want only the best for Your children.

Can Fear Cause Us to Serve Idols?

"The covenant that I have made with you,
you shall not forget, nor shall you fear other gods."
2 KINGS 17:38 NASB

The church paid the living expenses for a young woman with a special needs child. When her boyfriend moved in with her, the elders advised that the church wouldn't assist her while she lived in sin.

She argued that if she married the boyfriend, her government assistance for the child would cease. She trusted an amoral bureaucracy instead of Almighty God.

How often do we slide into this mindset? We work on Sunday instead of attending church, fearing our paycheck won't cover our expenses. We memorize song lyrics to amaze our peers instead of scriptures to glorify God.

Idolatry always brings adversity. The Israelites suffered calamity every time they turned away from Almighty God.

When we put our trust in the Lord, He will provide for our needs and deliver us from our enemies. He has always rewarded faithfulness, and He always will.

O Lord our God, help us to turn away
from empty idols and trust only in You.

Courage to Be Content

Give me neither poverty nor riches—feed me with the
food allotted to me; lest I be full and deny You, and say,
"Who is the Lord?" Or lest I be poor and steal,
and profane the name of my God.
Proverbs 30:8–9 nkjv

Our wages increase three percent, but our living expenses go up *eight* percent. We get a new car, but it loses value the minute we drive off the lot. A new medical treatment is FDA approved, but insurance doesn't cover it yet. The IRS refund check finally arrives, but they took part of it because of a mistake on the return.

If only we could orchestrate an even rhythm of our extreme highs and lows to the steady pulse of a heartbeat. But would we remember to thank the Lord in the ups and seek His support in the downs? These seesaw waves in life challenge us to be content regardless of the situations that come our way. Contentment comes only from the Lord.

Gracious God, let us follow Solomon's example to
trust in You no matter what our circumstances are.

Fear of Wicked People

The righteousness of the perfect shall direct his way:
but the wicked shall fall by his own wickedness.

PROVERBS 11:5 KJV

Some people seem to get away with their crimes. Even when overwhelming evidence points to their guilt. They should be indicted, prosecuted, and convicted. Lock them up and throw away the key.

They pull a few hidden strings and walk away unscathed, leaving a host of fearful victims in their wake of depravity.

What we don't see is their daily misery and bitterness. They have no joy as they use and abuse people on their path to a distorted image of success. When they reach their goal, they find a sterile emptiness. Their hearts have turned to lead, poisoned by their own malevolence. They sink into the mire of their own making, blaming others as they fail to perceive their wickedness.

These pitiful souls, blinded by their own vanity, desperately need prayer. Only the Lord can open their eyes to reveal His perfect way.

Righteous Father, we pray for changed hearts and cleansed
souls as we place our enemies into Your hands.

Fear of Worldly Influence

Then Jesus said to him, "Away with you, Satan!
For it is written, 'You shall worship the LORD
your God, and Him only you shall serve.' "
MATTHEW 4:10 NKJV

How presumptive of Satan to offer Christ what He already owns. The world and all that is in it belongs to God.

In his shrewd methods to lure us away from the Lord, Satan lies about the consequences of following his dark path. He doesn't disclose that a life of partying brings death by alcoholism, drug addiction, and disease. Enticements of "wealth by stealth" bankrupt our trust in each other. He says it's okay to lie, cheat, and steal. Everyone does it.

Jesus countered each of Satan's temptations with the Word of God. He gave us a powerful weapon to keep us in step with Him.

As worldly influences rush at us like water from a fire hydrant, let us deflect them against the Bible. Through prayer and studying the scriptures, we can submit to God's influence instead of acquiescing to Satan's world.

Gracious Lord, thank You for Your holy
word to fortify us against the devil.

Fear of God's Retribution

Samuel said to the people, "Do not fear. You have
committed all this evil, yet do not turn aside from
following the LORD, but serve the LORD with all your heart."
1 SAMUEL 12:20 NASB

In a discussion about Christian leaders, someone mentioned those who strayed from the faith and later returned. I confessed my own guilt at wandering away in the past. One thing I share with those well-known theologians is our triumphant return to the foot of the cross.

The Israelites experienced cycles of faithfulness to God, then infidelity to worship idols, then returning with shame.

God allowed them to be dispersed and held captive in foreign lands, the consequences of their sinful ways. But He granted them His forgiveness each time they repented.

I rejected the Lord in my youthful pride. Then adversity came, and I fearfully cried out to Jesus for help. The consequences couldn't be averted, but with a repentant heart, I leaned on Him throughout the difficulties. His loving forgiveness allowed me to return to the comfort of His bosom.

How blessed are we, Lord, whose transgressions You forgive!

Courage to Challenge
Wolves in Sheep's Clothing

*For many walk, of whom I often told you, and now tell you
even weeping, that they are the enemies of the cross of Christ.*
PHILIPPIANS 3:18 NASB

I listen to a pastor on the radio during my drive to work. In
his sermon on false teachers, he listed a famous TV preacher
among the many wolves in sheep's clothing. I had listened
to the TV "wolf" and came to the same conclusion. Yet this
pastor had the courage to speak out, naming names, despite
the consequences that might follow his broadcast.

The enemies of Christ aren't always obvious. The only way
to discern their false teachings is to study God's Word. Peter, in
his second letter, calls them springs without water. They avoid
the Gospel of salvation through Jesus Christ, even denying His
deity or virgin birth. They tickle ears with feel-good sermons
and water down God's wrath for unbelievers.

The radio pastor's boldness encouraged me to call out those
enemies of Christ.

*O, Holy and Righteous God, give us courage to challenge
those deceptive wolves by using the power of Your Word.*

Fear of Plundered History

If the foundations be destroyed, what can the righteous do?
PSALM 11:3 KJV

Moses received the law, written on stone tablets by the hand of God, yet this event isn't mentioned in world history. No class in our public schools teaches the account of the Ten Commandments.

In fact, in 1992, one Midwest state approved the purchase of new history books that claimed Napoleon won the battle at Waterloo, the atomic bomb was dropped on Korea, and General MacArthur, not Senator McCarthy, led the anticommunist campaign in the 1950s.

The Israelites failed to stand firm in their foundations and worship of God. As a result, no one knows the location of the ark of the covenant, which holds the stone tablets.

Like them, our history and our faith have been hijacked. We've allowed schools and society to erode the underpinnings of our faith and establishment of our nation.

We have the daunting task now, if we'll accept it, of convincing our culture that these two issues must go hand in hand.

Help us, Lord, to restore our foundations.
Let us once again live under Your righteousness.

Courage to Stand, Strive, and Suffer

But Joseph reported to his father some
of the bad things they were doing.
Genesis 37:2 TLB

"The sin of doing nothing is the deadliest of all sins," the Reverend Charles F. Aked said in his 1916 speech, in favor of prohibition.

Standing for a righteous issue, like Rev. Aked, takes courage. The deeper the controversy, the more proponents on both sides have at stake.

We'll strive against those who fear losing money or status, which might cost us our income or position.

We'll suffer more than indignation. Friendships and sometimes families are ripped apart. We might encounter property damage, slander, or personal threats.

Joseph had to stand, strive, and suffer. Giving Jacob a bad report about his brothers, he had to stand for his honesty. Striving against them, their plot to kill him landed him in an empty well. He suffered the loss of home and family as his brothers sold him to foreigners. Yet, he remained faithful to the Lord.

Righteous God, embolden us as You did Joseph in times when
we are called to stand, strive, and suffer for integrity.

Courage to Stand between the Devil and the Deep Blue Sea

But Moses said to the people, "Do not fear!
Stand by and see the salvation of the LORD
which He will accomplish for you today."
EXODUS 14:13 NASB

"Between the devil and the deep blue sea" is an idiom describing the choice between two possibly fatal situations.

Caught with Pharaoh's army before them and the Red Sea behind them, the Israelites panicked. Would they die by the sword of Pharaoh or drown in the sea?

But God provided a miraculous escape. He parted the sea with a strong east wind, and the people crossed to the other side on solid ground, not thick mud.

God freed us from the slavery of sin, yet we might panic when our old nature pursues us. An ocean of past failures blocks our escape.

God parted our deep blue sea with the red blood of Christ. We can come to Him, not through blood-soaked ground, but on the solid foundation of His name.

Merciful Father, You provided our miraculous escape through
Jesus. He shed His blood once and for all. It is finished.

Courage to Suffer for Righteousness' Sake

But even if you should suffer for righteousness' sake, you are blessed. "And do not be afraid of their threats, nor be troubled."
1 PETER 3:14 NKJV

We are targets for censorship if we dare to pray in Jesus' name in a public place. Unbelievers file lawsuits against us if we object to being forced to accept the world's immorality. Courts penalize us with steep fines for holding to our Christian convictions. These are frightening times, yes, but we aren't tied to posts in an arena filled with hungry lions. The early Christians endured significantly more than we have.

Jesus died a horrible death on the cross. Paul was beaten, stoned, and imprisoned for preaching about the risen Christ. The New Testament only records the fates of Judas and James, but most of the apostles were martyred for their faith.

As Christians, we will suffer. We will be tested, and our faith will be tried. We can endure only by holding on to Him who gives the crown of life.

As Christ suffered for us, O Lord,
give us courage to suffer for Him.

Courage to Live Like Saints

But as God is faithful, our word to you was not Yes and No.
2 CORINTHIANS 1:18 NKJV

In times of personal strife, I attempt to add humor to the dilemma by polishing my imaginary halo and referring to myself as "Saint Janet." Most people today equate saintliness with martyrdom, but Paul regarded all who believe in Christ as saints.

As Christians, we saints are expected to live with integrity. We reflect God's light in this world of darkness when we keep our word. Yet, unexpected crises often disrupt our day-to-day lives and delay or prevent us from keeping a promise. Even Paul was late in his promise to return to the church in Corinth due to unforeseen struggles.

Living like a saint takes courage as we juggle our integrity with our promises and afflictions. To maintain our integrity, we can only ascribe our setbacks to God's detours, and not to serve our own interests.

*Faithful Father, grant us courage in Your detours
to demonstrate Your grace and comfort to
help others and to live like saints.*

Fear of Betrayal

And He answered, "He who dipped his hand with
Me in the bowl is the one who will betray Me."
MATTHEW 26:23 NASB

Many of us bear invisible scars on our backs from the knives of false friends. The fear of betrayal can cripple our ability to trust others.

Considering Joseph, who suffered betrayal in the Bible, I searched for the reason God allowed it. Joseph's brothers betrayed him, and he became the foreman of an estate in Egypt. Then his master's wife betrayed him, which led to him becoming second in command of all of Egypt.

Then I thought about what good came from my own incidents of being betrayed. A disloyal coworker pushed me to seek a higher-paying job. An unfaithful fiancé forced me to seek—and find—a godly man, who became my beloved husband.

Jesus knew that Judas Iscariot would betray Him. Yet, trusting God's will, He understood the despicable act was necessary to bring about the crucifixion.

Dear God, as we endure the pain of betrayal,
let us remember that we can always trust
in You to bring about a good conclusion.

Fear of Deception

But I fear, lest somehow, as the serpent deceived
Eve by his craftiness, so your minds may be
corrupted from the simplicity that is in Christ.
2 CORINTHIANS 11:3 NKJV

The city of Corinth was known for rampant sin and idolatry, which concerned Paul. Would they be gullible to deceptive teachings?

Who is behind deception? What is the deceiver trying to hide from us? Why does he want to lead us astray? Where does he want to take us? When are we most susceptible to his trickery? How can we stand against this crafty adversary?

The serpent wants to conceal the truth about Christ's sacrifice. If we don't know what Jesus did for us, we can't share it with others. Bringing us to a state of confusion, he'll prod us to argue with each other instead of winning souls for God's kingdom. Misquoting God's Word, he tried to tempt Jesus when His body was weakened from fatigue, hunger, and thirst.

We can stand up to the deceiver through prayer and embracing God's word.

Holy God, when deception creeps in,
let the truth of Your Word banish it.

Courage to Keep Secrets

He who goes about as a slanderer reveals secrets,
therefore do not associate with a gossip.
PROVERBS 20:19 NASB

How easily we get pulled into the feast of gossip. It starts with one tasty little tidbit that grows until our mouths water for more juicy details. Courage to change the subject or just walk away doesn't come easy. We must be prayerfully prepared.

Working for a government contractor many years ago taught me the benign reply to prying questions: "I can neither affirm nor deny any validity to that allegation." Nosy people tried to trip me up by making inaccurate statements about my work or fellow employees. I struggled to push away the bait of correcting them so I wouldn't appear ignorant. The WWII expression, "Loose lips sink ships," helped keep my mouth zipped.

We can apply the same attitude when faced with the temptation to gossip. The Lord doesn't want us to sabotage another human being.

Dear God, when others trust us with confidential details,
give us the courage to embrace a new maxim:
"I've got a secret, and the Lord will help me keep it."

Fear of Moral Decay

The good influence of godly citizens causes a city to prosper,
but the moral decay of the wicked drives it downhill.
PROVERBS 11:11 TLB

Every generation since God wrote and gave His laws to Moses
has chipped away at the foundation of His laws. We've seen the
pendulum of morality swing back and forth over thousands of
years of human history.

In today's society, people scoff at the concept of purity in
mind and body. Standing firm in our ethical convictions brings
us under scrutiny and ridicule. Unbelievers wait with bated
breath for us to fall into a pit of sin.

Living under their vigilant appraisals, our attitudes, words,
and actions could be an influence of integrity to those around
us. When we pray, let us show our joy when God answers—
even for His "no" responses. When frustration comes upon us,
we can show our trust in God, proclaiming He is in control.

Righteous God, give us courage to influence people
in our midst to come to know and trust in You.

Courage to Fight for Our Faith

*"Do not be afraid of them; remember the Lord who
is great and awesome, and fight for your brothers,
your sons, your daughters, your wives and your houses."*
NEHEMIAH 4:14 NASB

Sanballat the Horonite, Tobiah the Ammonite, and Geshem the Arab conspired to attack the laborers on the Jerusalem wall.

Nehemiah prayed and assigned guards to protect the workers and the wall.

God answered by thwarting the attackers' plans.

The builders continued their work with a tool in one hand and a sword in the other.

Today, we face similar assaults against our faith. But our attackers come through the courts, legislators, and mass media. They pervert the law to demoralize our workers.

Fierce battles are necessary when our faith is challenged. Let us continue our Christian duties with our everyday tools in one hand, and the sword of the Lord in the other. We must protect our freedom of religion for the sake of those who follow behind us.

*Hear, O God, our prayer. We need Your
help in this fight for our brothers, our sons,
our daughters, our spouses, and our homes.*

Fear of Success

And the Lord replied, "I myself will
go with you and give you success."
EXODUS 33:14 TLB

We hide behind the door when opportunity knocks, afraid to answer.

Self-doubt of our inner strengths holds us back. Will we trade our moral values for success? Will we arrogantly flaunt our success to those trailing behind us?

We lack confidence in our skills. Or we could be sure of our abilities but not our motives.

Success usually means a new direction in life. Will we have to leave family, friends, and familiar territory?

All of these questions went through my mind as I sabotaged my brief acting career in my thirties. I answered them with other questions: *Is this what God wants for me? Could I honor Him in my self-centered performing arts profession?* Through my spiritual growth and study of the Bible, I can now rejoice in the new success He has provided to bring Him glory.

Dear God, let Moses' words be ours when faced with our
fears of success: "'If Your presence does not go with us,
do not lead us up from here'" (Exodus 33:15 NASB).

Courage to Fail

The Ten Commandments were given so that all could
see the extent of their failure to obey God's laws.
ROMANS 5:20 TLB

Peter, the apostle of Jesus Christ, tried, but failed to remain obedient to the Lord. He slept while Jesus prayed, cut off a soldier's ear, and then denied Christ three times.

We are flawed human beings, unable to yield our will to God's standard every day. Our imperfections prove that we can never be good enough to come to the Lord on our own. When we fail to follow His way, God's grace encourages us to get back in step again.

Like Peter, we will encounter failures along our Christian path. The Lord gives us the courage to overcome them so we can continue to grow in our faith, as He did for Peter.

God provided a standard to measure our obedience—the Ten Commandments. He didn't set us up to fail by creating an unreachable goal; He showed us we need Christ, the Savior, the fulfillment of the Law.

Heavenly Father, our failures weighed
against Your commandments attest to Your
abounding grace and forgiveness.

Courage to Have an Obedient Heart

But thanks be to God that though you were slaves of sin,
you became obedient from the heart to that form
of teaching to which you were committed.
ROMANS 6:17 NASB

Searching for a quick lunch with friends after church, someone suggested a local fast-food chain. Sudden change in plans—they're closed on Sundays. Monday through Saturday customers swarm the restaurant.

Our friend asked his employer for Sundays off so he could attend church. When the employer said no, the young man offered his resignation. It was a difficult step. He enjoyed the job and his coworkers, but he loved the Lord more. He honored the Lord not only with his work ethic, but also with his willingness to give it up to worship God. His boss took him off the Sunday schedule and kept him on the payroll.

As Paul praised the church in Rome for their obedience to the Lord in their struggle with sin, we can learn from their example. God always blesses our obedience to Him.

God our Father, give us obedient hearts to
courageously proclaim our love for You.

Fear of Job Loss

Lord, I have heard the report about You and I fear.
O Lord, revive Your work in the midst of the years.
HABAKKUK 3:2 NASB

Losing a job rarely happens when we can live without an income and benefits. It's difficult not to panic during this fearful time.

A company I worked for suddenly went out of business. As I walked away from the CLOSED sign, I passed a store window that displayed a print of two children on a bridge with an angel watching over them. Engraved at the bottom of the frame were the words "Trust in the LORD with all your heart. . ." My fears dissolved. I believed God would provide for my needs during this ordeal.

Habakkuk's example encourages us to look to the Lord with expectation, believing He will surely work everything out for us.

God has a plan for us. Perhaps not a job with a higher salary, but it will be an opportunity to praise Him for His faithfulness.

Gracious God, as we pray to be restored to work, let our fears
evaporate with the promise of Your guidance and provision.

Fear of Poverty

"For the poor will never cease to be in the land; therefore I command you, saying, 'You shall freely open your hand to your brother, to your needy and poor in your land.'"
<small>DEUTERONOMY 15:11 NASB</small>

Poverty results from either financial judgment errors or circumstances beyond our control. Sometimes we just can't get ahead. Job loss, auto repairs, medical costs, taxes, and fees all mount up against us.

Our fears grow like strangling weeds when we are unable to provide for our families. So we look for relief in high-interest loans, credit card advances, or gambling—and losing. Worldly solutions only serve to worsen our situations.

When we look to the Lord, praying with expectation, He will answer. Trusting Him for our sustenance opens wide the door to His supply.

The Lord didn't merely encourage charitable giving; He commanded it. And as such, He will use others in our godly family to provide assistance. They'll come with job offers, financial gifts, and groceries.

And His love.

Loving Father, give hope and courage to our brethren who live in poverty today. Show us how we can help them.

Courage Not to Sue

Actually, then, it is already a defeat for you,
that you have lawsuits with one another. Why not
rather be wronged? Why not rather be defrauded?
1 Corinthians 6:7 nasb

Trial lawyers' advertisements flood every sort of media. They encourage us to sue large corporations, small businesses, and even each other. Like lions feeding on a carcass, they promise a share of the compensation in a class action suit.

The apostle Paul urged the Christians in Corinth to consult a wise man among them to settle arguments instead of bringing their cases before the unrighteous courts.

Lawsuits between Christians show the world of unbelievers that we don't trust each other and, even worse, that we don't trust God to settle our disputes. Using Paul's solution, the two arguing parties can come together with an impartial elder to pray, discuss the issues, and resolve the differences amicably. And Christ is glorified in our love for one another.

O God, our Righteous Judge, give us the courage
to seek Your guidance in our disputes instead
of falling into the trap of litigation.

Fear of Wealth

"It is easier for a camel to go through the eye of a needle than for a rich man to enter the kingdom of God."

MARK 10:25 NASB

Jesus didn't say rich people wouldn't go to heaven. He said it would be hard for them to enter the kingdom of God if their love for money was greater than their love for Him. It's easy to wander away from our faith when we enjoy financial prosperity. Rarely do we cry out for help from the Lord when basking in success. Although that is a good time to give thanks.

God blessed Abraham with great wealth because of his faithfulness. Solomon asked only for wisdom and discernment, so the Lord rewarded him for his unselfishness.

Monetary resources enable us to support our churches, missionaries, and other Christians in need.

It isn't wealth we should fear, but our attitude toward it. Money in and of itself isn't evil. But whom do we serve: God or fortune?

God our Father, let us feed the hungry, clothe the naked, and shelter the poor with the riches You provide.

Fear of Financial Ruin

*But those who want to get rich fall
into temptation and a snare.*
1 TIMOTHY 6:9 NASB

Many foolish and harmful desires plunge men and women into ruin and destruction. Does anyone, besides the vendor, ever get wealthy from a get-rich-quick scheme? Selling instructional books or CDs is part of the marketing plan. The coaching materials usually collect dust on a shelf when they don't produce the desired results.

The threat of financial ruin is almost always the conduit that draws desperate people to the brokers of these schemes. The "low risk / high return" plans sound inviting. An occasional small gain persuades the investor to contribute more, only to get caught up in the trap of losing their initial capital. The financial ruin they feared will fall on them like an avalanche.

The best investment we can make when our financial failures seem imminent is in the Lord. He knows our situation.

*Father God, give us discernment to be good
stewards with our money and the courage to
trust You to carry us through financial ruin.*

Courage to Get Out of Debt

Owe no one anything except to love one another,
for he who loves another has fulfilled the law.
ROMANS 13:8 NKJV

In my grandparents' day, to offer credit was an insult. It suggested the patron's inability to pay for purchases. Now credit card applications come in the mail every day. So aggressive are the credit companies, that I received an application addressed to my cat!

The ease with which we can get and use credit cards makes them more tempting, until the bill arrives with taxes and fees added to the balance. Financial debt is legalized slavery. But being debt-free is a reachable goal with a sound budget and the courage to exercise self-discipline. Then all we'll owe is love!

Paul offered to pay any debt that Philemon's runaway slave owed. Isn't that a perfect description of what Christ did for us? Being enslaved by sin, we run away from God. The Lord Jesus Christ paid the debt that we can never repay.

Loving God, only through Your mercy and grace can our
offenses and debts be paid. And Jesus paid it in full.

Courage in Triumph

*For whatever is born of God overcomes the world. And this
is the victory that has overcome the world   our faith.*
1 John 5:4 NKJV

Corrie ten Boom said, "The first step on the way to victory is
to recognize the enemy."

In today's world, how do we recognize our enemy? He
doesn't wear a shirt with ENEMY emblazoned across the front.
I've never seen "I am your enemy—Hire me" typed on a business card.

The Bible clearly reveals our foes in Matthew 12:30 when
Jesus told the Pharisees, "He who is not with Me is against Me."
This describes most of the world. A force that large could be
frightening. But John reminds us that we have victory over the
world through Jesus Christ.

Protected by her shield of faith, Corrie triumphed over the
enemy with her Christian faith before, during, and after her
imprisonment.

Like Corrie, we celebrate a successful coup d'état with every
new believer we bring into the family of God.

*Lord, thank You for Corrie ten Boom, who identified Your
enemies and, in faith, claimed victory over them.*

Fear of Wars

"You will be hearing of wars and rumors of wars.
See that you are not frightened, for those things
must take place, but that is not yet the end."
MATTHEW 24:6 NASB

The first war in history occurred between two men: Cain and Abel. Since then, bitter conflicts have one trait in common: covetousness. Someone wants what the other has.

An assassination started the First World War—the proposed war to end all wars. The Treaty of Versailles brought it to a close. That pact severely punished Germany. Rebellion against the treaty's restrictions brought about World War II. When that conflict ended, hostilities persisted—not only in battlefields, but also in a cold war of suspicious envy.

Will we ever see the end of wars? The Book of Revelation describes the fulfillment of Christ's prediction. The last battle ends Satan's hold on us. When he is cast away for eternity, the curse of covetousness will go with him.

Dear God, thank You for providing this glimpse of future
peace. We take courage in the truth that You will be
victorious in the indisputable "War to End All Wars."

Fear of Peace

*"Peace I leave with you, My peace I give to you;
not as the world gives do I give to you. Let not
your heart be troubled, neither let it be afraid."*
JOHN 14:27 NKJV

Peace is defined as the absence of war or strife, a state of calm.
Yet a season of peace can be frightening. We miss the calm before
the storm while watching for thunderclouds of distress. Our
joy of peace is lost in constantly looking over our shoulders
and asking, "Will they attack today?"

There will be another attack, another battle, and another
war. Peace has been short-lived since evil entered the world.

Christ offers us the calmness of spirit that comes only
through Him. The world offers moments of tranquility, but
His gift of peace is eternal. Our hearts are free from trouble
when we keep our focus on the Lord. With Jesus as our ally,
why would we fear the calm before the storm? We know true
peace in the presence of our Savior.

*Father God, we seek Your peace every day
so our hearts will not be troubled, nor afraid.*

Our Wobbling World

God is our refuge and strength, a very present help in trouble.
Therefore we will not fear, though the earth should change
and though the mountains slip into the heart of the sea.
PSALM 46:1–2 NASB

Japanese engineers created a twenty-foot-high wall on the coast to protect them from imminent tsunamis. An earthquake opened a cavern under the sea, which dropped the shoreline approximately twenty feet. The ensuing tidal wave rushed far into the countryside, mocking their human efforts.

A volcano erupted in Europe, halting air transportation for days. Toxic clouds mingled with the weather pattern, making it too dangerous for airplanes to fly. Tourists and business travelers found themselves stranded in foreign countries.

The psalmist states that God is a very "present" help, which means He is always here to care for us, especially during earthquakes, tsunamis, and volcanic eruptions.

Dear Lord, You warned us that these geological instabilities
would increase in volume and intensity as the earth begins to
writhe in birth pains. By Your Word we know that You are our
refuge and strength. Let us look to You with hope and not fear.

Courage in Global Tribulations

"These things I have spoken to you, so that in Me you may have peace. In the world you have tribulation, but take courage; I have overcome the world."
JOHN 16:33 NASB

Explosions rip apart cities. Terrorist groups claim responsibility, hiding like cowards behind obscurity.

Bands of angry rebels use deadly force in their failed coup attempts.

A worldwide financial meltdown looms in the shadow of national monetary collapses.

These represent a few *Breaking News* stories that invade our homes every day.

These global tribulations could cause us to wring our hands in anguish, but Jesus didn't call us to live in fear. When we view these trials through His eyes, our hearts break for those who live in terror and hopelessness. We all have resources to help those in need to rebuild, if not physically and emotionally, then in sharing Christ's love. Even when our only recourse is to turn to the Lord in prayer, we find courage through our faith in Him.

Father God, fortify us as we kneel before You in prayer. We know You have conquered the tribulations of this world.

Courage to Heed Warnings

*So Joseph got up and took the Child and His
mother while it was still night, and left for Egypt.*
MATTHEW 2:14 NASB

An angel of the Lord alerted Joseph, in a dream, of danger to the Child. Joseph took his family and fled in the middle of the night.

God uses different means to warn us of impending threats.

A warning from the Lord can come as a powerful mental impression. A strong urge to take a different route to your destination might prevent an auto accident.

A salesman wants to enter your home. An uncanny sense of danger raises the hairs on the back of your neck. Close and lock the door.

I once dreamed of a tornado in my workplace. I had sensed strife and tension in my office during that week. God's forewarning led me to seek His guidance to prepare a resolution.

Whatever means God uses to alert us of threatening situations, let us gain courage from His warnings and take action, as Joseph did.

*Blessed Father, we find hope knowing You love
us enough to warn us of impending threats.*

Fearing the End of the World

"Heaven and earth will pass away,
but My words will by no means pass away."
MATTHEW 24:35 NKJV

The end will come. The Lord Jesus Christ predicted it. Every generation since His ascension has asked in fear, "Is the end really near?"

Only God knows the precise time it will occur. In His mercy, the Creator has hidden it from us. He knows we mortals tend to procrastinate and then panic.

Jesus provided advance warning in the scriptures. First, false prophets will claim to be Christ, misleading many. We will hear of wars and rumors of wars. Nations will come against nations. Then famines and earthquakes will increase. Knowing these are only the beginning of the end is frightening. How much worse could it get?

We can conquer our fears of the end by holding on to the words of Jesus—words that will never pass away.

O God our Creator, You have given us time to prepare our
hearts for the end. Let us use it wisely to share the Gospel of
the kingdom with the whole world, one person at a time.

Courage to Face Today

Wail, for the day of the LORD is near!
It will come as destruction from the Almighty.
ISAIAH 13:6 NASB

Today terrorists will choose new targets. They'll attack in the middle of the night, the middle of the day, the middle of a parade, or the middle of a race. But always in muddled secrecy.

Reports of violence come at us through mass media, including the Internet—not just daily, but minute-by-minute. Yet, if we look beyond the reports, we can find order in the chaos. Isaiah, among other prophets, warned of the great and terrible day of the Lord. As their prophecies unfold before us, let us look to the future day with courage.

Jesus said to the thief on the cross, " 'Assuredly, I say to you, today you will be with Me in Paradise' " (Luke 23:43 NKJV). Since we have Christ our Savior, we have no reason to fear the predicted day of the Lord's judgment. Like the thief on the cross next to Jesus, we will be with Him in Paradise.

Let today be the day, we pray, O Lord. Let it be today.

When Terror Strikes like a Viper

Do not be afraid of sudden terror, nor of trouble from the wicked when it comes; for the LORD will be your confidence, and will keep your foot from being caught.
PROVERBS 3:25–26 NKJV

During a clear Tuesday morning on September 11, 2001, terror gripped our nation by the throat.

Churches filled with people seeking hope. We asked God to heal the survivors, comfort the families who lost loved ones, and protect the heroes who searched the wreckage for victims. We prayed for the Lord's light to shine in our nation again.

This verse in Proverbs states *when* the onslaught of the wicked comes—not *if*. We live in a fallen world where evil people plot and scheme to terrorize the innocent. Fanatics continue their attacks throughout the world. We don't need to cower and wring our hands. We can open our Bibles and find courage in the treasure of God's comforting words.

O Lord God, our confidence remains in You before, during, and after Your enemies wreak havoc in this world. You are in our midst when terror strikes like a viper.

Follow the Courageous Child

"Truly I say to you, whoever does not receive the
kingdom of God like a child will not enter it at all."
MARK 10:15 NASB

Jesus embraced the children brought to him and praised their simple, innocent faith.

Our friends took their nine-year-old grandson with them on a mission trip to a small European nation. In a quaint village he found some boys playing baseball in a field. They invited him to join them. He noticed they had no shoes, and his heart broke for them. He gave one boy the shoes off his feet. Each child coming up to bat took his turn wearing the shoes.

The family returned to the United States, and the grandson approached his pastor about sending shoes to the children of that village. The Sunday school classes joined in the shoe drive ministry. A nine-year-old child made an everlasting impact for Christ on a group of boys playing baseball. It spread to their families and to the village through one initial act of kindness.

Father, when we lead our children to Christ,
prepare us to follow their courageous footsteps.

Fear of Drought

I cared for you in the wilderness,
in the land of drought.
HOSEA 13:5 NASB

We often envision a drought as dry, cracked, infertile ground. But it's much worse. A drought can devastate an entire region, bringing famine, disease, war, and death.

A drought of the heart is equally devastating. We hunger and thirst for fulfillment. When none comes, bitterness makes our hearts sick. We declare war on God and suffer the death of hope.

God succinctly describes this progression in the Book of Hosea. We pray to Him when we suffer a drought. It could be financial, emotional, or spiritual. God answers our prayers with green pastures. We rejoice and praise Him. Then we become satisfied.

In our satisfaction we become proud. Our self-righteousness overshadows our thankfulness.

When we become proud, we forget how He cared for us in that hour of need. Our growth is stunted, bringing us back to drought. Our only hope is to return to the Lord.

Dear God, You give us living water through Jesus—
a well that will never run dry. Protect us
from our own droughts of the heart.

Courage in Flooding

*"I will remember My covenant, which is between Me
and you and every living creature of all flesh; and never
again shall the water become a flood to destroy all flesh."*
GENESIS 9:15 NASB

Driving through a thunderstorm, I sighed with relief when the
storm clouds retreated behind me. Then I realized the streets
in my neighborhood would be knee-deep in water.

I glanced across a field on the other side of the highway and
beheld a perfectly shaped, perfectly hued rainbow. My fear of
seeing my street turned into a lake when I got home evaporated.

That rainbow changed my perspective. It reminded me to
pray for the people in flooded Iowa and Texas, as well as the
hurricane victims along the Eastern Seaboard.

Our old wood-frame home, built on a hill, had never
succumbed to the flooding that normally accompanies heavy
rains. The rising water in my street might have been annoying,
but it wasn't life threatening.

*Dear God, thank You for sending colorful reminders
that You keep Your promises, and for prompting
us to pray for others in harm's way.*

Courage in the Eye of the Storm

*But when he saw that the wind was boisterous, he was afraid;
and beginning to sink he cried out, saying, "Lord, save me!"*
MATTHEW 14:30 NKJV

Aside from the obvious—wind, lightning, thunder, and precipitation—stormy weather can also represent looming ominous conditions.

Jesus knew His disciples would run into a storm when He ordered them across the Sea of Galilee. He also knew that persecution hung over their future ministry.

As Jesus approached them on the stormy sea, only Peter had the courage to get out of the boat. By faith, he could walk on water—not calm, smooth-as-glass water, but rising waves from tempestuous winds. Peter sank when he allowed his surroundings to distract him. He cried out to the Lord, and Jesus saved him.

In calming the storm, Jesus taught the disciples who He was, is, and ever shall be. This lesson in faith prepared them for the assaults they would face, even after Jesus' death, resurrection, and ascension. Let it prepare us, too.

*Dear God, grant us courage to call on
You in faith as we tread our stormy seas.*

Fear of Riding Out the Storm

He said to them, "Why are you fearful,
O you of little faith?" Then He arose and rebuked
the winds and the sea, and there was a great calm.
MATTHEW 8:26 NKJV

Police woke my friend at 3:00 a.m. A hurricane was headed toward the coast. They ordered everyone living at the beach to evacuate.

As she loaded her pets and essentials into her car, her neighbors refused to go. Someone might break in and steal their possessions. She told them hurricane-force winds carried more danger than looters. A storm surge could wash them away, along with all they owned. Fears of staying or leaving paralyzed them.

Riding out our personal storms can be just as frightening. Emotional tidal waves, financial windstorms, or marital tornadoes can blow into our lives without warning. Sometimes, professional help offers an evacuation route. In other instances, our only option is to hunker down until it blows over. In either case, Jesus is with us. He alone has power over the winds of turmoil.

Heavenly Father, let us take shelter in
You as we ride out our fearful storms.

The Courage to Evacuate

I would hasten my escape from
the windy storm and tempest.
PSALM 55:8 KJV

In Psalm 55, David wrote about escaping the tempest of his enemies and treachery of a friend. In Florida, our worst enemy is a hurricane. Unlike a tornado, which gives little warning, a hurricane's slow movement offers us plenty of preparation time.

When Hurricane Charlie set its eye on Tampa, my husband and I secured our home as well as we could. Then we planned our evacuation route. It seemed everyone on Florida's west coast headed toward Orlando in the center of the state. We packed up the car with clothing, groceries, and our two cats, then headed north.

While we spent a peaceful night in Alabama, Charlie skipped Tampa and cut a northeasterly path across the state, heading straight for Orlando.

Like David's deceitful friend in this Psalm, Hurricane Charlie betrayed the multitude who thought they'd fled to safety.

Gracious Lord, our weather can be as fickle as false friends,
but we know You will never betray us. You stay with us,
even when we head straight into the storm.

Courage against Demonic Presence

*Because greater is He who is
in you than he who is in the world.*
1 JOHN 4:4 NASB

An oppressive bleakness weighed heavily on my heart as I sat at my computer, writing my devotions. Then my spine tingled. The hairs on the back of my neck rose. I hadn't experienced an evil presence before, yet I knew in my soul that a demon invaded my workspace. Fear closed in, as if to smother me.

Demons envy and hate us humans. They sealed their fate by choosing to follow Satan. But God created us a little lower than the angels and provided redemption for our sinful choices.

The Bible calls Satan the slyest of all creatures, so I chose not to match wits with one so crafty. Instead, I called on Christ to rebuke and send the evil spirit away. He answered my plea, and the overwhelming peace of the Holy Spirit replaced my fear.

Lord God, we can courageously stand against demons when we call on You, for You are greater than anything in the world.

Fearing Spiritual Warfare

Then Michael, one of the top officers of the heavenly
army, came to help me, so that I was able to break
through these spirit rulers of Persia.

DANIEL 10:13 TLB

Our earthly wars cannot compare to the combat raging in
the spirit world. A twenty-one-day struggle delayed the angel
responding to Daniel's prayer. That angel enlisted Michael's
help to overcome his evil opponents.

The devil and his demons gave up their home in heaven
when they dissented against God. Satan appears to be stepping
up the pace of his vile attacks because he knows his period of
influence is growing shorter.

We catch an occasional glimpse of his warfare if we pay
close attention to fearful events—from worldwide tensions to
family conflicts. But the apostle John's vision of the battle in
Revelation 12 gives us courage. We know the Victor of that war.
Our Father's goodness always triumphs over evil.

Dear God, we know by Your Word that we need not fear
spiritual warfare. Let us take comfort in our faith that
You have already prevailed against the adversary.

Fear of Lost Communication

But I, like a deaf man, do not hear; and I am
like a mute man who does not open his mouth.
PSALM 38:13 NASB

My husband went into panic mode one Sunday evening. "I can't find my phone." Missed calls could mean irate clients.

I frantically searched the house, while he looked in the car and walked the length and width of the yard.

I used my phone to call his but didn't hear the distinctive ring tone he'd set up for me. He'd silenced it during the church service and forgot to turn it back on. My locater app showed his phone was at our location. But we had looked everywhere, hadn't we?

Finally, I peeked under our sleeping cat's blanket. She yawned, stretched, and blinked at me as I pulled the device out from under her. "Is this yours?"

My husband ducked his head and admitted he now remembered dropping the phone on the bed while changing clothes.

Gracious God, we fear being technologically deaf and mute
when separated from our devices. But that fear diminishes
when we hear and speak Your Word—the Bible.

Courage to Cross Bridges

"And besides, there is a great chasm separating us,
and anyone wanting to come to you from here is stopped
at its edge; and no one over there can cross to us."
LUKE 16:26 TLB

The overpass I use daily on my drive to work rises high in the air. Each time I reach the upward span, adrenaline rushes through my veins.

This fear comes upon me at the point where I see only the sky above and the pavement in front of me. At this juncture, I lose my bearings. The panic fades when the span levels out, and I see the highway. My bearings have returned as quickly as they'd fled.

We all must cross the great chasm that separates this earthly life from eternity. In Luke 16, Jesus described only two destinations after death: the comfort of Abraham's bosom and the flame of agony.

I may lose my bearings on the overpass, but because of Christ's sacrifice, I am sure of my eternal destiny.

Gracious Father, although I lose my point of reference
in my daily drive, Jesus is my compass for heaven.

Fear of Fear Itself

The fear of man brings a snare,
but whoever trusts in the LORD shall be safe.
PROVERBS 29:25 NKJV

Franklin D. Roosevelt stated these memorable words in his 1933 inaugural speech: "The only thing we have to fear is fear itself." Four months later, panicked citizens pulled their money out of banks. Mass hysteria arose from their fear of fear itself.

The men who helped Caleb and Joshua check out the Promised Land said they felt like grasshoppers in the midst of giants. Their fear blinded them to the greatness of God.

Phobophobia is the fear of a phobia. A panic attack develops at the thought of coming across the feared object. My dread of downtown soured my stomach before I got in the car. But urgent business demanded my attention. I prayed for God to diminish my fear of traffic, one-way streets, and limited parking. He answered as I paid the meter and walked two blocks to my destination, my fear fading with each step.

Father God, help us remember that we can overcome
the unreasonable, unjustified terror that paralyzes
us—only by placing our trust in You.

Fear of Heights

*"Is not God in the height of heaven? And behold
the height of the stars, how high they are!"*
JOB 22:12 KJV

Fear of heights, like most immobilizing phobias, is partially rooted in not having control of our environment. The higher the elevation, the denser the breathable air. A loss of balance causes vertigo.

Another part of this fear might be from our quest to reach God. Climb the tallest tree; the heavens are higher. Take the elevator to the top of the Willis Tower in Chicago; the heavens are higher. Scaling the jagged cliffs of Mount Everest; the heavens are higher. Soaring toward the moon in a NASA rocket; the heavens are higher.

No matter how far above the ground we get, the heavens will always be above us. We can't reach God through our own works. In His great love for us, He came down as Jesus of Nazareth, to dwell with and suffer for His creation.

*Heavenly Father, calm our fears of the high places.
Let us feel Your embrace in our lowly place here on earth.*

Fear of Flying

How precious is Your lovingkindness, O God! And the
children of men take refuge in the shadow of Your wings.
PSALM 36:7 NASB

Twenty-five million Americans share aerophobia—the
fear of flying. This condition can also be associated with
claustrophobia—the fear of cramped spaces, agoraphobia—the
fear of being trapped, and acrophobia—the fear of high places.

I once preferred to fly only at night to avoid seeing the
ground thirty thousand feet below. Fewer passengers traveled
at night, so I felt less like a sardine.

The Psalms offer many comforting verses that calm those
nagging fears. They assure us that God's lovingkindness extends
to the heavens. His faithfulness reaches to the skies. He has
displayed His splendor above the heavens. And my personal
favorite: "The heavens are telling of the glory of God; and their
expanse is declaring the work of His hands" (Psalm 19:1 NASB).

As we board an airplane, we find courage under God's wings
through reading His Word.

Heavenly Father, Your Word tells us that the heavens
are Yours, the earth also is Yours; the world and
all it contains, You have founded them.

Courage to Travel

While they were talking and discussing, Jesus Himself
approached and began traveling with them.
LUKE 24:15 NASB

Some people suffer from hodophobia, an intense dread of travel. This fear isn't always associated with a specific means of travel, such as airplanes, but with the significant distance away from home. It could be related to an earlier, harrowing travel experience that hasn't yet been overcome. News reports of terrorist attacks and road rage incidents add to the trepidation.

Cleopas and his friend had good reason to fear traveling on the road to Emmaus. Jesus had been crucified, dashing their hope of a redeemed Israel to shattered pieces. But when He joined them—incognito—they boldly explained everything they knew about His death and resurrection.

Jesus revealed Himself to them as He broke the bread with them, and they traveled back to Jerusalem to share their experience with the eleven.

When fear hinders our travel plans, let us consider the opportunities, as Cleopas had, to boldly tell someone about Jesus.

Gracious God, please grant us courage to conquer
our fears of travel, for You always go with us.

Fear of Confined Places

*When He had said these things, He cried out
with a loud voice, "Lazarus, come forth."*
JOHN 11:43 NASB

I was fifteen when my claustrophobia first appeared. A friend wanted to see how many of us could fit inside her VW Bug. I climbed into the backseat. Others pressed in around me. I couldn't breathe. I screamed and pushed with all my might at those near me. The next thing I remembered was standing on the sidewalk with a circle of friends staring at me wide-eyed. Where did I get that superhuman strength? Fear has its own muscle.

Confined inside a closed space, like an elevator, feels like being trapped alive in a tomb. Imagine Lazarus's reaction to Jesus calling him out of the tomb four days after he died. Death was no match to the power of Christ. Martha expected a stench but saw the glory of God instead.

Nothing is too big for our Lord—not even a small, confined space.

*Heavenly Father, as Jesus was there to free Lazarus,
we know He's here to release us from our tombs of fear.*

Fear of Clowns

A joyful heart makes a cheerful face,
but when the heart is sad, the spirit is broken.
PROVERBS 15:13 NASB

My friend is terrified of clowns. She views them as frightening imposters or interlopers who mask their identity with painted faces. The news media and film industry add to her fear as they capitalize on scary clowns.

It might calm her if she realized how much we're like clowns.

We mask our broken hearts with laughter. We paint our faces with expressions acceptable for the moment, instead of revealing our true feelings. I've known people who hide their own fear by striking fear in others around them.

We do this because we want to be accepted, or we don't want pity. We feel vulnerable when we show our true selves.

Happy clown, sad clown, or scary clown—which face do we allow people to see? God can give us the courage to reveal the real person beneath the face paint.

Gracious Lord, You know who we really are,
and still love us. Help us learn to share our
broken hearts as easily as we share our joys.

Fear of Ethnicity

There is neither Jew nor Greek, there is neither
bond nor free, there is neither male nor female:
for ye are all one in Christ Jesus.
GALATIANS 3:28 KJV

When God dispersed the people at the tower of Babel, different ethnicities developed as they adapted to diverse climates. Xenophobia quickly followed. The devil wants to divide and conquer us through hate. God wants to join us together in one spirit of love.

In Jerusalem, the Romans despised the Hebrews. The Hebrews shunned the Samaritans, and the Samaritans steered clear of Gentiles and Jewish people.

Jesus didn't view the Samaritan woman he spoke with as a foreigner to shun, but as a person who needed His gift of eternal life. Many in the city of Sychar believed in Christ because of His brief conversation with a woman drawing water.

God sees us as one people through Christ. As soon as we believe in Jesus, we become joint heirs according to the promise.

Gracious Father, with Your love, we can view others
through Jesus' eyes, either as Christian brothers and
sisters, or people who need Your gift of eternal life.

Fear of Deep Water

"Water encompassed me to the point of death."
JONAH 2:5 NASB

While vacationing on a Caribbean island, I strolled to the end of a nearby dock that extended out into the turquoise water. Being a so-so swimmer, even the deep end of a pool frightened me. Sheer determination to overcome my fear gave me the courage to climb down the ladder and dog-paddle a few feet to a huge boulder.

Up to my chest in the Caribbean Sea, the water was so clear I could see my feet on the boulder. I also saw the ocean floor fifty or so feet below it. Short, panic-filled breaths robbed my lungs of oxygen. I thought of Jonah's plight and prayed for courage. When I looked down again, I marveled at the water's clarity. It magnified the bottom making it appear much closer. For the first time, I viewed my terror of the deep through fearless eyes. Even in the depths of the sea, God is with me.

Lord God, Your truth comes to us even through our fears,
if we will only look to You in those moments.

Fear of Crowds

When Jesus noticed how large the crowd was growing, he instructed his disciples to get ready to cross to the other side of the lake.
MATTHEW 8:18 TLB

Some people believe agoraphobia is an irrational fear. But there are valid reasons to fear crowds. Spread of contagious viruses, pickpockets, and other thieves waiting to steal our money or identity. We don't dare let go of our child's hand in fear of "stranger danger."

Getting caught up in a throng leaves us with no directional control. We can't locate the exits, or we find ourselves separated from our people. Recent terrorist bombings at crowded events have put us on alert. It's prudent to be aware of our surroundings.

There is a stronger reason *not* to fear crowds. Jesus didn't suffer from agoraphobia. Crowds formed everywhere He went. He offered them His pearls of wisdom and, in doing so, left an example for us. Let us use every opportunity to share God's love in a crowd of strangers. . .with words, if necessary.

Lord, You are our protector. We put ourselves in Your hands as we bravely minister to the multitudes.

Fear in Sensory Overload

They saw it, then they were amazed;
they were terrified, they fled in alarm.
PSALM 48:5 NASB

In a large, crowded store, background music competes with screaming babies and the buzz of multiple conversations. Beeping registers join the discord as cashiers scan product codes. Signs, labels, and small-screened infomercials throughout the store try to grab our attention. Aisles blocked by workers stocking shelves and customers' carts impede shopper traffic.

With all the distracting interference, I can't focus on my errand. Sensory overload is a bubbling brewery for panic. More than once, I've had to leave my cart and escape the chaos, feeling defeated.

Mount Zion was an imposing sight with palaces, towers, the Temple, and bustling people. Was it sensory overload that frightened away the kings in Psalm 48, fleeing in defeat? Or perhaps the fact that God was the city's stronghold. Either way, God reigns.

Great are You Lord, and greatly to be praised. In the
moments of panic when I suffer from sensory overload,
give me the courage to focus on one sense at a time,
and to trust You to bring me through the frightening ordeal.

Fear of Blood

"For this is My blood of the covenant, which is
poured out for many for forgiveness of sins."
MATTHEW 26:28 NASB

Since bleeding is often a sign of something wrong with the body, some sense of fear at the sight of blood is normal. However, when we add weakness and fainting to an increased heart rate, perspiration, trembling, and nausea at the sight of a pinprick, we probably suffer from hemophobia. As with other phobias, it is usually rooted in a previous traumatic experience—exposure to gory horror movies or the bloodshed of war.

I wonder if Pharaoh developed this fear after Moses turned the Nile to blood. That event must've been traumatic for the Egyptians.

How did King Solomon keep from fainting at the dedication of the temple when he sacrificed so many sheep and oxen they couldn't be counted? His prayer of praise to God brought him joy.

Dear Lord, thank You for the new covenant through the blood
of Jesus Christ. When we feel faint at the sight of blood, let us
rejoice that the blood of the Lamb has washed away our sin.

Fear of Roaches—AKA Palmetto Bugs

> "'All the winged insects that walk
> on all fours are detestable to you.'"
> LEVITICUS 11:20 NASB

In Florida, we refer to large roaches as palmetto bugs, so named because they breed in palmetto bushes.

My husband would stomp them with his shoe, while I prefer to empty a can of insecticide on each one—after my initial heart-stopping scream.

In my opinion, these scary creatures, which God pronounced unclean and detestable, epitomize sin. They hide in the dark, scurrying away when exposed to light. Like sin that creeps into our lives, we wonder how they invade our homes when they appear in all their disgusting and frightening vileness.

How do we handle sin when it surfaces in our midst? Do we crush it, pulverizing every remnant? That will eliminate one incident, but it won't prevent an infestation. Saturating it with the Word of God not only exterminates it, but also repels any future entry when used at every portal.

Dear Lord, as we protect our homes from
unclean insects, help us to rely on Your Word
to protect our lives from detestable sin.

Fear of Snakes

*"And as Moses lifted up the serpent in the wilderness,
even so must the Son of Man be lifted up."*
JOHN 3:14 NKJV

When my friend who is afraid of snakes and lizards saw a snake eat a lizard, she admitted to feeling torn. Symbolically, her greater fear devoured the lesser one.

Is a fear of snakes rational because of the serpent's role in the fall of mankind? God uses all critters to demonstrate His plan.

Chapter 21 of Numbers relates how the Israelites grumbled against the Lord. When He sent fiery serpents, the people confessed their sin, and Moses prayed to the Lord to remove the venomous snakes.

The Lord commanded Moses to create a symbolic serpent and set it on a pole. Anyone who was bitten could look at the raised serpent and live.

Jesus used this to foretell His death on the cross. If everyone who is bitten by the curse of Satan looks at Jesus and believes in Him, they shall live.

*Lord God, please replace our fear of snakes with the image
of Christ, lifted up, in His victory over the sly serpent.*

Fear of Spiders

"So are the paths of all that forget God; and the hypocrite's hope shall perish: whose hope shall be cut off, and whose trust shall be a spider's web."
JOB 8:13–14 KJV

Aside from a severe allergic reaction to spider bites, my dread of multi-legged creatures is rational. In my opinion, they represent Satan's deceptiveness. The spider's eight legs make determining its direction nearly impossible.

Satan hides his wayward course in his schemes of confusion, fear, or temptation. He weaves his webs of distractions to lure us away from the love of our Lord. His paths lead only to pain and hopelessness.

As children of the Most High God, our hope will never perish. We might get caught in the devil's divisive webs, but our heavenly Father is always here to lead us back to the paths of righteousness.

A spider sighting now reminds me to turn my eyes back to Jesus. Nothing Satan has to offer can match the wonderful love of my Savior.

Lord, thank You for providing reminders to keep us on Your path where our hope shall never be severed.

Fear of Worms

But I am a worm and not a man,
a reproach of men and despised by the people.
PSALM 22:6 NASB

Worms once repulsed me, until I learned about this exceptional creature.

In Psalm 22, David used the Hebrew word *tolaath* to describe himself as a worm, but not an ordinary worm.

The tolaath, or Crimson Worm, climbs onto a tree or other wooden post to deliver her young. While laying her eggs, she secretes a dark red fluid that stains the tree and covers her with a shell to protect her offspring. She then dies to give them life.

After the third day, her protective shell turns from crimson to white. In death, her head and tail are pulled together forming a heart. Another sign of God's eternal love.

Jesus Christ is our Crimson Worm, the tolaath, who covered our sin with His blood and washed us white as snow with His love. Is it any wonder He quoted Psalm 22 from the cross?

O God, thank You for David's wisdom to tell us
about the Crimson Worm—a preview of Your
wonderful plan of salvation for mankind.

Fearless Lizards

The lizard you may grasp with the hands,
yet it is in kings' palaces.
PROVERBS 30:28 NASB

Lizards range in size from a two-inch anole to a ten-foot Komodo dragon.

Since Agur, the author of Proverbs 30, included the lizard among the small creatures that represent wisdom, it's obvious he wasn't writing about the Komodo. Some biblical scholars state the Hebrew word is translated as chameleon or gecko.

This little reptile benefits us by feeding on a variety of insects such as cockroaches, spiders, beetles, and flies. In a way, it provides a God-sent pest control service.

So why, then, did Agur feature a lizard in his list? Though small and insignificant, it has the confidence to enter the palace and approach the throne of the king without fear.

This little creature symbolically shows us that, although we are small and insignificant in the vastness of God's creation, we can boldly approach our King of kings. The fearless lizard has taught us to be fearless indeed.

Lord God, You use a tiny creature to remind us we
can draw near to Your throne of grace without fear.

Fear of Medical Professionals

"This, at least, gives me comfort despite all the pain—
that I have not denied the words of the holy God."
JOB 6:10 TLB

Overzealous surgeons nearly crippled my mother while treating her constant pain. Each operation should've eliminated the hot poker searing down her leg. Instead, her suffering intensified.

I asked God why my mother had to endure more than a decade of agony at their hands. He reminded me that Jesus had to suffer an excruciating death on the cross for me. . .for my mother. . .for the world He loves.

God doesn't always heal pain and sickness in the manner we choose. He looks deep within us to determine which needs the most healing—the physical ailment or the broken spirit. Like Job, in all my mother's misery, she didn't give up her faith in Christ.

For many years, I feared doctors and nurses because of their inability to relieve my mother's affliction. With the Lord's help, my fear and distrust of medical professionals is steadily diminishing.

Holy God, remind us to pray for, not fear, medical professionals
as they make difficult life-and-death decisions every day.

Fear of Pandemic Diseases

*"Or if I should send a plague against that country
and pour out My wrath in blood on it. . ."*
EZEKIEL 14:19 NASB

No disease existed in God's perfect world. But Adam's sin perverted the healthy environment God created. Since then, new diseases have emerged with deadly consequences.

The Black Death mushroomed from China to India to Persia to Syria and to Egypt. Twenty million Europeans died after trade ships brought it to Italy. People back then believed God delivered this plague as punishment for their sin. Did they know the Lord's warning in Ezekiel of a plague against His people for their idolatrous sin? Perhaps they remembered the Angel of Death passing over those who had the lamb's blood on their doorposts.

The deadliest plague we face today is the spread of agnosticism. While biological diseases might take lives, the sin of unbelief can take souls. The Word of God is the only healer.

*Almighty God, help us to put the blood of the Lamb on
the doorposts of our hearts to protect us while we spread
the Gospel of Jesus Christ throughout the world.*

Fear of Sleep

The fear of the Lord leads to life, so that
one may sleep satisfied, untouched by evil.
PROVERBS 19:23 NASB

Ah, sleep. A most wonderful time of rest. . .except when frequent violent awakenings jolt the sleeper out of a peaceful dream.

It began when my husband grabbed my arm in the middle of the night with the urgency of someone going over a cliff. Although he had no memory of the incident, he apologized, saying he felt light-headed. I eased back to sleep, only to have the ordeal repeated an hour or so later.

I asked if he had nightmares. He denied having any dreams at all.

The incidents escalated, and he bruised my shoulder.

We prayed for guidance as our fear of sleeping grew with each new injury.

When he broke my finger, a friend recommended a neurologist who diagnosed, and, eventually, put an end to my husband's unconscious attacks. He had developed a rare form of epilepsy. Seizures only occur when the patient is asleep.

Heavenly Father, thank You for Your answer to our prayers that
we both could once again sleep satisfied, untouched by evil.

Dread of Funerals

But I do not want you to be ignorant, brethren,
concerning those who have fallen asleep,
lest you sorrow as others who have no hope.
1 THESSALONIANS 4:13 NKJV

I was five years old when Granddaddy T. K. died. Someone at the funeral picked me up and held me over the casket. The ashen face I saw bore no resemblance to my beloved granddaddy.

The reception with relatives and friends at our home after the funeral brought some comfort. Listening to the happy stories the adults told, along with viewing family photographs, eased my fear of the dead man in the coffin.

In a cloudless sky, a clap of thunder shook the house. A relative shouted joyfully, "He made it!"

We had no doubt Granddaddy was in heaven. He believed in Christ and accepted the gift of eternal life He promised.

And I learned that my granddaddy looked different in the coffin because he was no longer in that body, an empty shell that once housed his soul.

Gracious Lord, we honor our loved ones with funerals.
Knowing they are with You turns our sorrow into hope.

The Dreaded Diagnosis

"For I am the LORD your God, who upholds your right hand,
who says to you, 'Do not fear, I will help you.'"
ISAIAH 41:13 NASB

Stage Four Renal Cell Carcinoma.

My husband and I looked at each other, shocked. Stage Four? How could his disease advance that far unnoticed? The radiology report had to be wrong. The only symptom occurred the week before, but the cancer had already spread.

This terrifying news came eighteen months after his epilepsy diagnosis. The symptoms of that disease were so incongruent we feared he had Alzheimer's. The neurologist stopped the bizarre seizures through medication. As long as we maintained the right dosage, our medical worries were over. Or so we thought.

Through surgery, ensuing radiation, and immunotherapy drugs, we continued to cling to the Lord for hope.

Each new scan brought another dread of diagnosis. Is the cancer under control? Has it grown? Whatever the next scan showed, God reminded us through His Word that He would be with us all the way. We will not fear.

Holy God, holding Your loving hands, we have
the courage to face each new diagnosis. Thank You.

Fear of Hospitals

And I know this, that whatever God does is final—
nothing can be added or taken from it; God's purpose
in this is that man should fear the all-powerful God.
ECCLESIASTES 3:14 TLB

We presume hospitals are sterile, yet unclean hands took my father's life. We don't know if an employee or a visitor delivered the septic infection. He was too young to die. His untimely death left me afraid of hospitals.

Years later, my husband needed a life-saving operation. His surgery required him to stay a full week. Although the facility was miles from where my father died, my fear tried to dominate my judgment.

The staff washed their hands and changed gloves every time they tended to my husband's needs. A private room resolved my concern about visitors' germs. The Lord showed me a hospital functioning as it should and dispelled my fear.

Why did God provide this level of care for my husband, but not for my beloved father? We can't comprehend His sovereignty, for He ordains our steps for His purposes.

All-powerful God, give us courage
to accept Your ways in faith.

Courage in an Emergency

My voice rises to God, and I will cry aloud;
my voice rises to God, and He will hear me.
PSALM 77:1 NASB

That evening seemed like every other evening. My husband had supper on the stove when I came home from work.

While I changed from my office clothes to casual rags, he went to lie down for a few minutes. His fight with cancer wore him out.

He struggled to exhale, emitting a loud groan. His eyes rolled back in his head.

I called 9-1-1.

Red lights of an ambulance flashed in front of my home before I could get the door unlocked. A platoon of paramedics raced to the bedroom. A prayer floated around somewhere in the back of my mind.

As they transported my husband to the hospital, I found courage in the knowledge that God hears and answers us when we cry out to Him.

Thank You, Lord, for our first responders. They are trained to fight fires, fight crimes, and fight death. You have given them hearts of compassion and wisdom to come to our aid.

Courage to Let Go

*"Then God released him from the horrors of death
and brought him back to life again, for death
could not keep this man within its grip."*
ACTS 2:24 TLB

I watched the echocardiogram technician press her wand against my husband's chest.

He suddenly flat-lined.

A stampede of people in scrubs rushed to his CCU room.

Someone pulled me from his bedside. At that moment, nothing was more frightening than watching them take turns performing chest compressions on my husband.

The doctors later said that my husband had died three times in two days, being brought back to life each time.

Tears blurred my vision. I took my adult stepdaughter's hand and told her, "If the Lord wants him that much, we have to let him go."

In that decision, the hardest we've ever had to make, the Lord gave us peace. He released my precious husband from the horrors of this mortal life, along with its diseases.

Because of my husband's faith in Christ, he is finally home.

Heavenly Father, give us courage to let our suffering loved ones go into Your dwelling place to worship at Your throne.

Fear of Loneliness

Turn to me and be gracious to me,
for I am lonely and afflicted.
PSALM 25:16 NASB

When my husband would leave the house for an evening meeting, I didn't feel lonely. I knew he would return in a few hours. That certainty comforted me.

He traveled out of town for a week to help a friend. The fear of loneliness crept up on me. The house felt empty. Then he called to let me know he'd arrived safely and would be home soon. I knew I would see him again in a few days.

Several years later, as paramedics transported him to the hospital, deep despair closed in around me. The house creaked in our shared solitude.

His condition quickly declined, and he went home to be with the Lord.

With the power of God's promise, I pushed back the dark loneliness that overshadowed my broken heart. Wrapped in the Lord's embrace, I know I will see him again in Heaven.

Dear God, You are a gracious companion to all who fear You.
Thank You for Your comforting embrace in our darkest moments.

An Unnamed Terror

My heart is in anguish within me,
the terrors of death have fallen on me.
PSALM 55:4 NIV

After my husband's unexpected death, his briefcase remained in a chair, pushed to a corner of the kitchen, for a couple of months. Bills, receipts, and tax information huddled inside. Every time I went near it, an immobilizing terror overcame me. Like a force field in a sci-fi movie, fear repelled my efforts to open the briefcase.

I couldn't understand my unfounded terror of this simple item. Identifying the cause is the first step in conquering any fear. I prayed for the Lord to reveal the cause to me. A phobia is an irrational dread of having no control. My fear wasn't about *not* being in control, but *being* in control.

My husband handled our finances. Taking control of his briefcase meant I was now in charge. In my distress and sorrow, I didn't want to be. I looked to God for help.

Gracious Lord, as we grapple with our mysterious fears,
You give us the courage to name them, face them,
and overcome them.

Courage in the Face of Death

We are of good courage, I say, and prefer rather to be absent from the body and to be at home with the Lord.
2 Corinthians 5:8 nasb

How do we stare down an enemy as menacing as death?

Although God created us to live forever, death entered the garden when the Lord had to kill an animal to cover the sins of Adam and Eve. They were then evicted, lest they eat of the tree of life. He loves us too much to let us live eternally with the stain of rebellion separating us from His grace.

I've stared down that old enemy in the loss of my parents, relatives, close friends, and my beloved husband. Each time, I took comfort in the Lord's loving embrace and the knowledge that, because they believed in Jesus Christ, they prefer to be absent from the body and present with the Lord.

Gracious God, thank You for giving Your Son, Jesus, to vanquish the last enemy on the cross. We who believe in Him won't be separated from Your love when we leave this earth.

Fear of Uncertainty

Why are you in despair, O my soul? And why have you become disturbed within me? Hope in God, for I shall again praise Him for the help of His presence.
PSALM 42:5 NASB

After my husband's unexpected death, I feared the uncertainty of my future without him. The most daunting task I had to assume, after twenty-one years and six days of marriage, was our finances.

Adjusting from a two-income couple to a one-paycheck widow dangled a concrete block of distress over my head. Would I have sufficient funds to stave off the creditors? Would I lose my home? In my despair, I cried, and then I prayed.

The Lord reminded me of the widow who cried out to Elisha, fearing a creditor would take her children. Elisha showed her how God would multiply her resources.

To others who fear this uncertainty after the loss of a spouse, I will offer a gentle suggestion: cry, pray, and watch the Lord work His miracles.

Gracious God, Your provisions are as great as our faith and obedience. I praise You for the calming help of Your loving presence.

Fear of Added Burdens

Cast your burden on the LORD, and He shall sustain you;
He shall never permit the righteous to be moved.
PSALM 55:22 NKJV

Our cat Pixie ministered to my husband during his illness. Every morning before leaving for work, I would kiss him goodbye and say a quick prayer. Then he'd go back to bed for a brief rest. The cat tucked him in with her treading paws and gave me a confident expression that said, "I've got this, Mom."

Two months after losing my husband to cancer, Pixie became ill. Now, he was gone, and it was my turn to minister to her.

My financial struggles, busy workload, writing deadline, and now an ailing kitty knocked the strength out of my weary mind and body. A friend, trying to comfort me, said, "God never gives you more than you can handle."

But He does.

If we could handle these added burdens, would we cry out to Him for help?

Loving Father, when we cast our fearful burdens on You,
You are faithful to answer and cover us with sustaining peace.

Courage to Be Sad

*Sorrow is better than laughter,
for sadness has a refining influence on us.*
ECCLESIASTES 7:3 TLB

When my sister's firstborn son was a small tyke, he came home from school with a song, "It's okay to cry. Sometimes you *feeeeeel* better." His little voice rose an octave on the word "feel."

The memory of his sweet song comforts me when my daily tears come. At first, I tried to stifle my sorrow. We're supposed to keep a stiff upper lip and not let grief get in the way of our lives, even in the death of a loved one. Yet, every weekday at four o'clock, I begin to cry. That was the hour my husband would call me at work to ask what I wanted for supper.

Solomon's wisdom revealed that sadness brings healing to the heart. Tears cleanse the soul of grief. So, I pray for the courage to be sad. It's okay to cry, it really does make me *feeeeeel* better.

*"My soul weeps because of grief; strengthen me
according to Your word" (Psalm 119:28 NASB).*

Courage to Be Joyful

Sing praise to the Lord, you saints of His, and give thanks at the remembrance of His holy name. For His anger is but for a moment, His favor is for life; weeping may endure for a night, but joy comes in the morning.
PSALM 30:4–5 NKJV

"Don't be sad; be happy!" But what makes us happy or sad? How long does it last? Both are temporary emotions that can't exist without good or bad news or good or bad times. Praise from my husband made me happy, but his momentary anger made me sad. Being by his side, whether in his praise or anger, made me joyful.

Joy doesn't depend on good or bad news, or times. We can be joyful even when sorrow surrounds us. If we cry ourselves to sleep at night, joy awakens us with the dawn. When worry weighs down our hearts, knowing God holds us in His hands lifts us up in joy.

We can smile through our tears or sing praises to the Lord in our courage to be joyful at all times.

Loving God, thank You for joy!

Courage to Finish

*I have fought a good fight, I have finished
my course, I have kept the faith.*
2 TIMOTHY 4:7 KJV

I accepted my assignment with great hope that someone
would find blessings in my work. I labored night and day,
giving up weekend fun with my husband and friends. Small
interruptions hindered me at first. As they escalated into more
serious obstacles, I realized that the evil one didn't want me to
finish this project. When the Lord suddenly opened His gates to
welcome my husband into heaven, I crumbled under profound
grief and considered quitting. But God's tender promise, "I will
help you," urged me onward.

Even as Paul knew death crouched at the door for him,
he encouraged Timothy to fulfill the ministry of Jesus Christ,
even unto hardship.

God gives us emboldened strength when we need it most.
Losing my husband so suddenly ripped everything I had out
of my heart, but the Lord filled it back up with His unending
love, giving me the courage to finish.

*Most precious loving Father, I have finished
this course. I have kept the faith. Thank You.*

Scripture Index

Special Editions of the My Prayer Journal

My Prayer Journal: Quiet Moments for Busy Days

What better way to guarantee a good day than to spend time in prayer? *Quiet Moments for Busy Days* encourages women to set aside just a few minutes each day for quiet time with God. Dozens of topically arranged, faith-building prayers are accompanied by inspiring devotional thoughts and encouraging scripture selections.
Spiral Bound / 978-1-63409-693-5 / $7.99

My Prayer Journal: Mornings with God

What better way to guarantee a good morning than to spend time in prayer? *Mornings with God* encourages women to do just that—to set aside just a few minutes each day for quiet time with God. Dozens of topically arranged, faith-building prayers are accompanied by inspiring devotional thoughts and scripture selections from the beloved King James Version of the Bible.
Spiral Bound / 978-1-63409-697-3 / $7.99